ALL THE LITTLE MONSTERS

DAVID A. ROBERTSON

ALL THE LITTLE MONSTERS

HOW I LEARNED TO LIVE WITH ANXIETY

HarperCollins*PublishersLtd*

HarperCollins Publishers Ltd
Bay Adelaide Centre, East Tower
22 Adelaide Street West, 41st Floor
Toronto, Ontario, Canada
M5H 4E3

www.harpercollins.ca

Library and Archives Canada Cataloguing in Publication

Title: All the little monsters : how I learned to live with anxiety / David A. Robertson.
Names: Robertson, David, 1977- author.
Description: First edition. | Includes bibliographical references.
Identifiers: Canadiana (print) 2024051677X | Canadiana (ebook) 20240518276 |
    ISBN 9781443472401 (softcover) | ISBN 9781443472418 (Ebook)
Subjects: LCSH: Robertson, David, 1977-—Mental health. | LCSH: Illness anxiety disorder—
    Patients—Canada—Biography. | CSH: nêhinaw—Biography. | CSH: Swampy Cree—Biography.
    | CSH: First Nations authors—Biography. | CSH: Authors, Canadian (English)—21st century—
    Biography. | LCGFT: Autobiographies.
Classification: LCC RC552.H8 R63 2025 | DDC 616.85/250092—dc23

Printed and bound in the United States of America

24 25 26 27 28 LBC 5 4 3 2 1

The sensitive issues discussed in this book, including suicidal ideation, may be triggering to some readers.

You can't go back and make a new start, but you can start right now and make a brand-new ending.

—James R. Sherman, *Rejection*

[Anxiety] is something that is part of me, but it's not who I am.

—Emma Stone

CONTENTS

FOREWORD

David Alexander Robertson first entered my life in 2015 on a CBC Radio program I hosted and co-produced about writing in Canada. We had a series highlighting authors with exceptional skills and enough output to be able to reflect on a body of writing: essentially an acknowledgement of lifetime achievement. Usually, the writers I spoke with for this series were in their seventies, at the very least. David wasn't even forty, but he had written more than a dozen graphic novels and had just published his first novel-novel, if you will, *The Evolution of Alice*.

In our conversation, David told me he first knew he wanted to be a writer when he was in grade three. That was when he wrote his first book, which he still has in his possession. About a hundred pages in to *All the Little Monsters*, he reveals the charming title, so I won't name it here. From that early start, David has grown into a wonderful storyteller. Both his output and his talent are prolific. David uses his prodigious gifts to create understanding, to share the truth of the history and contemporary reality of Canada, and, of course, to tell a powerful story, all culminating in creating community.

Outside of the radio studio, David and I connected on a number of levels: we both have ancestral roots in Norway House, Manitoba; we both love driving around Winnipeg with a curated soundtrack; we both love dad jokes; and we both live with challenges to our mental health.

Throughout my four-decade career at CBC Radio, I was sometimes known as "Mary Sunshine." I sounded cheerful. I radiated cheerfulness. I had a laugh once described by the journalist Marcia Kaye as "rich and hearty and sweet but with a touch of sin, like a plum pudding in a bubbling brandy sauce." She added: "of course, not everyone likes plum pudding." The comedian Mary Walsh, dressed as super-shero Marg Delahunty, Princess Warrior, and followed by a camera crew, once burst into my live on-air studio to smite me with her sword and say "Shelagh Rogers, you're so sweet you make my teeth ache." Much as I loved (and still love) Mary Walsh, I had just found out a friend had died and I didn't have the capacity to play along. I replied, "Go to hell, bitch." It may have been the most real I had ever been on air up to that point. And it lasted two seconds.

I knew I wasn't sweet. I wasn't permanently cheerful. And I wasn't plum pudding. The relentless (Mary) sunshine was a false front, a facade, an overcompensation for . . . for . . . something I couldn't express or understand until 2003. That was the year I was diagnosed with clinical depression after a mental (what they called at the time a "nervous") breakdown.

Breakdown sounds like it could mean a kind of dance, or something that happens to toys or cars. I searched for a definition, and a doctor told me it's a "non-medical term used describing a time-limited event that presents primarily with debilitating depression, anxiety, or paranoia."

What that meant, in my case, was losing interest in everyone I loved and everything I cared about. What had seemed so important for so many years just didn't matter, didn't even register. I lost the ability to function day to day and became completely oblivious to personal hygiene.

Off the conveyor belt of work, I felt hopeless, helpless, worthless . . . name your "less." I had, and not for the first time, thoughts of suicide. My general practitioner referred me to a psychiatrist, who diagnosed me with clinical depression. I kept that a secret.

Officially, the CBC said I was on a "stress leave." I said my time away from work was due to extreme hypertension (my blood pressure was in fact very high: 180/110). In an article in the *Globe and Mail* on February 1, 2003, Dr. Gabor Maté wrote: "the ebullient radio host insisted, 'It is not a stress leave. It is because I have high blood pressure.' Ms. Rogers may be excused for making that false distinction. In keeping with the mind/body split endemic in Western culture, the medical profession itself fails to recognize—despite ample research evidence—the connection between the stresses of modern life and elevated blood pressure. Insufficient attention is paid to stress reduction as a way of treating high blood pressure."

I love and respect Dr. Maté, even though he busted me back then. I had ignored stress, thinking that's what got me out of bed every morning. I worked through, or I thought I did, the blues, the blahs, and the clouds. Until I couldn't because my own little monsters started sucking my energy and passion dry, like Nancy Crater, the shape-shifting salt vampire in an early *Star Trek* episode.

Had there been a book like *All the Little Monsters* in 2003, I would have understood what I was dealing with—that it wasn't weakness (the journalist and mental health advocate Michael Landsberg really called it when he said he was "sick not weak") and, so importantly, that I wasn't alone.

The book you are holding is a treasure. David Robertson, my friend Dave, is wide open, unflinchingly honest, and brave. So brave. I think of Terry Gilliam's cut-out animations for *Monty Python's Flying Circus*, specifically of a man whose forehead flips open, allowing us to see everything inside his head. Dave shows us what is in his head and on his mind. He shows us what is in his heart, too, both physically, as if the reader were part of the crew on the miniaturized submarine the *Proteus* in the film *Fantastic Voyage*, and emotionally, his words reaching into our own hearts like the transcendent songs of Jeremy Dutcher. Dave acknowledges the role of his family in keeping him in solid mental health and in being there for him: his dad and his mom, his five children, and the scaffolding that is his wife, his great love and lifeline, Jill. It is so important to recognize those who care for us, especially when the little monsters are whispering lies into our ears. "Little monsters" is the perfect analogy for mental health illness, and, as Dave says, "whatever those little monsters are saying to you, they are always lying, no matter how convincing they sound."

Back to our very first conversation almost ten years ago. Dave told me he thinks his best writing comes when he's writing about difficult subjects. This book proves him right. Gratitude for Dave's candour, his courage to speak his truth, and for building belonging. *All the Little Monsters* is for us.

—Shelagh Rogers

ALL THE LITTLE MONSTERS

THE MONSTER SPEAKS

I was alone in my hotel room.

It had been a tough week. I was at a writers' festival in Calgary, about to go onstage for a panel about mental health, which I'd been writing about more often over the last few years. There was no particular reason why the week had been hard. Sometimes, there's a clear explanation, and I can trace my destructive thoughts or awful body sensations to an event or a stressor; I suspect this is true for many people. I may be overtired, overworked, emotionally exhausted, and so on. Stuck in the moment, I can't see the forest for the trees. I can't sift through the fog. Other times, there doesn't seem to be a reason; my mind and, in turn, my body decide they're going to wreak havoc on my life. My anxiety seems to come out of nowhere. For me, at least, it happens when I've let my guard down. I may have had an uncharacteristically great week where I felt close to normal; I may have caught myself thinking, *Hey, maybe it's gone, maybe I'm just . . . okay*, and then I'm hammered with it in the worst way, as if it wants to remind me that it's here forever.

That I'll never be free from it.

I'd forced myself through several busy days at Wordfest, which was full of school visits and other events. When I could, I retreated to my room to rest, but I would think, worry, and analyze every little thing going on in my body, and there was no rest in that. And now, only minutes remained before I had to meet the other panellists in the hospitality suite on the hotel's first floor. I was pacing back and forth in my room, doing what I'd been doing whenever I found myself alone that week, when I opened the balcony door and stepped outside into the fresh air.

It was autumn, and a crisp and cool breeze was sauntering by. I caught it against my face and closed my eyes for a moment to try to enjoy the sensation, to try to live outside of my anxiety, if only for a second. I heard scuttling, as if a mouse were walking by my feet, and I opened my eyes to find the origin of the sound. A dried autumn leaf had found its way onto my balcony, and with the help of the quiet wind, it was tiptoeing across the concrete, where it would inevitably get caught up in the air and continue its journey, no care in the world.

I looked down as though I could see where the leaf had come from, which tree had let it go, but I ended up staring at the ground. And a thought came and went, quick as a lightning bolt, and in its celerity, hard to articulate.

My hotel room was several floors from the ground level. I pictured the sidewalk. I imagined walking with my fellow panellists down the street towards the library where the event would take place. I had to take the elevator to get down there, and it flashed across my mind how much quicker it would be if I stepped over the edge and fell like an autumn leaf. It was not the first time a thought like this had announced itself, and falling was not the only method of my suicidal ideation (in fact, falling was a rare thought because I'm afraid of heights), but whatever modus I'm considering, it's always quick. I suppose, luckily, or sometimes unluckily, my fear of death trumps my fear of life. At any rate, like every other time, the image of my death and of silencing my anxiety, panic, and depression came, and it went. On this occasion, it was ushered away by a telephone ring; the party was about to leave for the library, and I had to hurry downstairs.

I took the elevator.

When I entered the hospitality suite to gather with my fellow panellists and members of the Wordfest team who were walking over to the event with us, I, like I'd done so many times that week, pushed my anxiety to the side so that I could put on a face, so that I could function in a social environment. I greeted everybody as the fun, relaxed guy I'd learned to put forward, and we left the hotel en route to the library, an easy five-minute walk away.

It was a nice walk. I hadn't seen Alicia Elliott, a Haudenosaunee writer, in a while, nor Shelagh Rogers, a long-time broadcaster and Métis with roots in my home community, Norway House Cree Nation. We caught up with each other during the brief hike. The company, the chilly air, the traffic, and the thought of the event all distracted me from the unpleasant sensations I had been hiding in my body. I felt better than I had all week. Then, as we passed a restaurant I frequented while in Calgary, a panic attack hit me with the force of a truck. I was blindsided.

The relative quietness in my body gave way to an all too familiar chaos.

What was the trigger? What set me off?

I couldn't think of an answer. I couldn't think of anything that had kicked my mind and body into overdrive. And yet, there I was. There it was. My anxiety, that little monster, coming in to give me a terrible embrace. I talk about my anxiety as though it's a living being; it's hard not to think like that when it's with you so often and for so long.

Anxiety manifests itself in different and disparate ways, from person to person. It can be a pervasive sense of dread, and you may know the source of the terror or not; it may be just a feeling that something awful will happen, and you feel a certainty about that. You may feel butterflies, the kind an athlete gets before a big game, or a public speaker before stepping out in front of a large crowd; only there's no game and no crowd. Your mind might race so quickly that your thoughts smash together like cars in a freeway pileup, blocking everything else so that all you have are those thoughts, and you don't know how to make sense of them or how the mess will be cleared. For many people like me, there is a physical reaction with varying degrees of severity. Headaches. Sweating. Stomach problems. Shortness of breath. Shakiness. Weak knees. Rubber legs. Dizziness. Hives. Numbness in your extremities. Chest pain. That's why, at my worst, I called an ambulance because I thought I was having a heart attack. Twice. And it's why I've developed acute hypochondria (I'm not sure if that's a thing; I just, perhaps appropriately, made up my condition and diagnosed myself); it can make you feel anything and everything and often several symptoms at once.

Anxiety can be an onslaught.

I felt a few of those things while walking with the crew past the restaurant, but most notably, as the case had been for me for the last while, my heart began to "skip." I had a flare-up of PVCs, or premature ventricular contractions. I put *skip* in quotation marks because when you experience PVCs, your heart is not skipping; it's beating twice in short order, which disrupts the heart rhythm, and a pause follows those quick beats. People describe the uncomfortable sensation as a flutter. Everybody has them at some point, but lucky people never feel them. During a panic attack, my heart welcomes an extra beat, every beat, so that all I feel are flutters and skips, and I feel Every. Single. One. And so, while lumbering to the library, I began to deep breathe, one of the techniques I use to dull anxiety and panic, while simultaneously trying to keep up a conversation (and not let on I was having a panic attack) and ignore my heart, which was going haywire.

You're not going to die. You're not going to die. You're not going to die.

I made it to the library's front steps, the first of several flights that would eventually bring us to the second floor, where the event would take place. I always make it, no matter how awful I feel, no matter how positive I am that this time will be the one, that I'll collapse to the ground, shrivel up, and be carried away like the leaf that had found its way onto my hotel room balcony. But even though I always make it, sometimes I'd rather not. I'd be okay with not. But this evening, I had a job to do, and I did what is typical of me: I added a new line to my internal chant.

You can do this. You can do this. You can do this. Fuck you, anxiety.

*

Stairs became a problem for me years ago, when my PVCs turned frequent, and, gradually, I allowed my anxiety about them to prevent me from taking part in strenuous exercise, then moderate exercise, and then exercise altogether. It's a frequent joke in my family that I haven't sweated for five years, but it's not a joke. I haven't. When I see a flight of stairs, even the stairs that lead up to the second floor of my house where my bedroom is, I hesitate for a split second (or longer).

I think, *What if I go up the stairs, and halfway up, my heart gives out?*

There aren't even a lot of steps in my house. If an escalator breaks at the airport and I have to take many steps, I catch myself looking for an elevator. Or I start thinking about what the last thing I said to my family was because those will be the last words they'll hear from me. Did I tell them I love them? I've been to the Memorial Park Library on several occasions for Wordfest, been to the second floor and got there via the stairs, and I know there are a shitload of steps, first from the sidewalk level to the first floor, then from the first floor to the second. With my heart nonstop skipping, notwithstanding other damage the panic attack was inflicting on me, I looked up to the top of the stairs, to the front door of the library, and thought, *You can't do this.*

It's difficult for me to believe that I have a mental health illness; it's far easier to accept that I have a physical ailment, because there are treatments that can provide a cure for that. I can't count how many times I've asked my therapist, my doctor, or my wife, Jill, "Can anxiety do this?" The answer, of course, is that anxiety absolutely can. It's a sickness of the mind, and the mind controls the body. It's an easy equation, but it's frustratingly hard to admit to myself. I often think of how much farther along I would be in my mental health journey if I could acknowledge that very thing: I am on a mental health journey. Why can't I recognize it? Because if I did, it would be an admission: I'm sick in my mind, not necessarily in my body.

If I were to be honest with myself, I would say, with relative certainty (some conditions have been officially diagnosed, and the existence of others are impossible to deny), that over the last fifteen years, I've lived with (I always catch the words *suffered with* before they find their way out of my mouth, or onto the page) generalized anxiety disorder (GAD), health anxiety, depression, panic disorder, and obsessive-compulsive disorder (OCD). Jill says that's why I have to eat breakfast by a specific time, as well as lunch and dinner, and if I don't, I start to freak out. That's also why I take my pills at precisely 7:00 a.m. (metoprolol), 8:00 a.m. (alprazolam), 2:00 p.m. (alprazolam), 7:00 p.m. (metoprolol), and 10:00 p.m. (bupropion). I'm not sure how productive it is to be this exacting. I don't think it would change anything if I weren't. Prescription medication often necessitates regularity—i.e., take one pill twice per day, twelve hours apart—but not down to the minute. And if you miss a dose, depending on the drug, you can usually take it when you remember or wait until your next dose with little, if any, harm done (this is what I have been told by a pharmacist). This fixed schedule, I suppose, is a way to find some control when it feels like there is so little I can control.

It's easier for me to admit—perhaps it's a concession—that you can have physical and mental ailments simultaneously. What I mean is that I can live with health anxiety, and those worries can be founded; as in, I can really be physically sick. In those cases where I am ill, anxiety compounds the physical ailment. As I was writing this section, literally writing the words *You can do this*, my heart began to beat in a rhythm so irregular that my Kardia device (something I should *never* have gotten—people with health anxiety should never own something that affords them the ability to assess their symptoms, even a thermometer) labelled my pulse as *unclassified*, which is not an uncommon finding; it could mean an arrhythmia, a fast/slow heart rate, or just a poor recording. But to me, it may as well have displayed *You're fucked*.

Unsurprisingly, I panicked, which made my heart even more irregular, and within half an hour, I was in the emergency room at Grace Hospital, near my home in Winnipeg, where triage ordered an ECG stat. The triage nurse was worried because she read my heart rate as being under forty beats per minute, and I looked like Casper, which isn't good for a Cree guy with dark olive skin. As it turned out, my heart wasn't beating under forty times per minute, but the extra beat was so close to my regular beat that it read as one beat. I was having PVCs every single beat. I went to the hospital at 2:00 p.m. and was home by 6:30 p.m. because there wasn't anything they could do for me. I knew it. Jill knew it. But I went anyway. That monster of mine kept whispering in my ear that I was dying. I've gotten better at ignoring him, but I listen more often than I would like. And so, one day later, here we are. I'm back at the computer, still alive, taking it one moment at a time and doing my best to ignore the butterflies flittering inside my chest.

We're back at the library.

I looked up at the stairs and thought, *You can't do this*, but in this instance, I realized it was my anxiety talking, and I didn't listen to it. I climbed the stairs with the other panellists one step at a time. I made it to the front doors of the library, conquered the next flight of stairs, stopped on the landing with Shelagh to find the sketches of us Wordfest had commissioned (a welcome rest before taking on the challenge of the last flight), and then made it to the second floor. We were led into the green room, a charming space with a table in the middle, surrounded by countless books and a jar of cold water with a collection of empty glasses. I took one, filled it, and drank some water, waiting for my heart to find its normal rhythm. By then, it had become obvious to the others that something was wrong. I'm pretty good at hiding a panic attack, but sometimes, you just can't. It was likely that my skin tone gave me away; I probably, like the day at Grace Hospital, looked like Casper. I told the group that I was in the throes of a panic attack. And then, at that moment, we were visited by a surprise guest: Naheed Nenshi, the then mayor of Calgary.

I'd not met him before, and when I shook his hand and exchanged a few words, I tried my best not to let on what I was going through. Nenshi stuck around for a few minutes. He was as awesome as I expected him to be, and then he left the room. As soon as he was gone, the head of the festival, Shelley Youngblut, and the panellists tended to me. They were amazing. I know them all: Shelley, Alicia, Shelagh, and Sarah Leavitt, a graphic novelist. They're great people, and they weren't strangers to mental health conditions, so while two alprazolam tablets dissolved on my tongue, they made sure I was okay. Alicia asked me if I needed to stay in the green room.

"We got you," she said.

I considered it. I was in shambles. But that was the point. I needed to go onstage in shambles and tell people I was in shambles so that if anybody in the audience was in shambles too, they would know, like me, that it was okay.

It was okay not to be okay.

"You sure?"

Yeah, I was sure. Minutes later, I walked onstage, still in the middle of the panic attack (the alprazolam not having had enough time to kick in yet), but with a support group both on the stage and in the crowd.

Shelagh, our moderator, threw it over to me first, asking how mental health had affected me personally.

I decided to let the audience know what I had been, and what I was, going through.

"Quite significantly," I said with my anxious voice, something only Jill can recognize. "You never know when someone's struggling. I posted a picture on Instagram a few months ago about a festival I was at in Lethbridge, Alberta, and to look at the picture, you wouldn't think that anything was up. But during the picture, I was having a panic attack. And I was actually having a panic attack in the room before we came on today. And so, it's affected my life quite significantly. It was about ten years ago that I had a nervous breakdown. A lot of things had happened . . . one day I was coming from work, and I stopped at a pharmacy and I checked my blood pressure, and it was through the roof, so I went home and called the public health line, Health Links, and they told me to call an ambulance. I went to the hospital, and they sent me home with some lorazepam, and I couldn't get out of bed for about a month."

I went on, I dug deep—we all did—and when it was over, it wasn't an event anymore; it was a community. My heart settled. The panic subsided. And while I knew that my heart would skip again, and I knew that I'd have another panic attack, I knew, as well, that talking about it and sharing my experience with others was something I had to do going forward. And I have. Since that time, I've had struggles, I've had triumphs, I've felt strong, I've felt weak, I've felt like a hypocrite, I've felt like a mentor, I've made connections, and I've told my story repeatedly. And now I'm sharing it with you.

Writing this book has become inevitable. Writing this book has become a necessity. Because my journey cannot fit into a sixty-minute lecture or an op-ed. It cannot only be borrowed from, in pieces, to fill out the plot of a supernatural murder mystery I'm writing. The more I've talked about my struggle with mental health, the more I've come to understand where it began, how it grew into what it is today, how I've learned to cope with it, and how I've come to accept that it will always be a part of my life. This memoir shouldn't just refer to little monsters in the title. Those pesky creatures on my shoulders should be the co-authors.

But I suppose if they were, it would mean that I've ceded control to them—and that's not the case. As often as I fuck up and listen to them, it is me who is at the wheel, not them. I have to know that; it's not enough to believe it. I have to understand that this is my story, not theirs.

ONE
I COULD SEE FOR MILES

Mental health is a journey, and it's not a day trip. It's lifelong. I've yet to hear somebody say that they are cured of their anxiety or depression or anything that falls under the umbrella of mental health. As far as I'm concerned, once you have it, you have it. That can be an intimidating thought, and I get it. When I look to the future, I often feel discouraged knowing that when I'm sixty, when I'm eighty (if I make it that far—that's my fear talking), I'll still be living with my anxiety. I often tell Jill I can't imagine living like this for that long. Then, if I'm objective, I acknowledge that I've lived with the worst parts of it for fifteen years already. What's thirty more? Plus, when I think back over the past decade, it's the good stuff I recall, not the bad. It's like my brain filters it out for me, like experiencing it once was enough. Maybe it'll always be like that. My goal is to live with anxiety more and more productively. To refuse to allow it a voice in the story of my life. To reduce it to an annoying airplane neighbour reading my work over my shoulder as I write a chapter thirty thousand feet in the air. They can read my words, but they don't get to tap the keys.

My father once said you don't know where you are unless you know where you've been. And, when you know where you are, you know, as well, where you need to go, and you can figure out how to get there. You can apply this to anxiety. You don't truly understand it unless you know where it started. When you understand its origin, the monster becomes less frightening. But more than that, you can see how living with it for an extended period is possible—and that maybe, just maybe, it doesn't have to be such a grim outlook.

It would be easy for me to point to the time, in 2010, when my world crashed down on me. A lot was happening in our lives. I switched jobs, we moved houses, my daughter Lauren was born, my grandmother died, and my mind and body said, "You're done." I could point to the middle of that summer and say that's where it started, but the reality is, that was just when everything came to a head. I can follow a path from 2010, when I was thirty-three, back to my childhood. The seeds of my anxiety and my depression were planted then, and without realizing it, I nursed those seeds for decades until they finally burst.

We are time travellers. We visit the past—the events and decisions in our lives—sometimes repeatedly. Typically, these trips to another time are powered by regret, things we wish we would have done differently. For example, I was a good basketball player but never tried out for a university team, so I'll never know if I could have made it. Why didn't I? I picture myself walking on, having an amazing tryout, and making the Winnipeg Wesmen. I wish I had tried. It will always bother me that I didn't, and I'll never understand my reasoning back then. It bothers me even more as I age, and playing basketball at any level becomes unlikely. I may act like I'm still young, but my body doesn't seem to agree with my level of maturity.

When I used to visit my father in his study, I often found him sitting in his recliner, staring out the window.

"What're you doing?"

He was also a time traveller. In the years leading up to his death, he spent a lot of time thinking about his youth. But his journey to the past wasn't due to regret; Dad never had much use for that counterfactual emotion.

"You can't change the past."

My father had learned through Story while living on a trapline, had learned in his first and only language, Swampy Cree, in a land-based, experiential environment for nearly ten years. Then, when he left the trapline and subsequently attended a day school in Norway House Cree Nation, he had to learn differently, and in English, not Cree. To accomplish this, he found it easier to leave the things he'd learned in his early years behind. In his young mind, there was no way to translate the knowledge people like his grandfather had gifted him into this new language. Years later, as an Elder, he made it his mission to figure out a way to draw on the teachings of his youth and apply them to his life. He was teaching others from that place of discovery. Others like me. Reclaiming things that have been lost seems more worthwhile than thinking about things that cannot be changed.

If you let go of regret, you can learn a lot from the past. The trick is learning to recall a moment and not manipulate it but stay in it, observe, and listen. Figuring out how to do that has, in turn, helped me understand the root of my anxiety.

I was young, but old enough, at least, that Michael, one of my brothers, and I had stopped sharing a room in the house I grew up in in Winnipeg. Cam, my oldest brother, had moved into the basement, which freed up the room that I moved into. I have a lot of memories in that room. Cam once pretended to be the boogeyman after I'd read *Night Shift* by Stephen King, hiding in my closet for a long time until leaping out at just the right moment and scaring the shit out of me; that terrifying prank took dedication that only a big brother could have. I listened to my first CD in that room: Ugly Kid Joe, *Menace to Sobriety*. I used to listen to Winnipeg Jets games on the radio with my ghetto blaster while lying on the floor, erupting into cheers each time Curt Keilback announced a goal or a big save by Bob Essensa. On that same ghetto blaster, I listened to oldies while trying to fall asleep at night.

I had trouble falling asleep. I thought listening to old music would help me, but it never did. I can still remember, with great clarity, listening to "Hang On Sloopy" or "Leader of the Pack" with my eyes wide open, staring at the ceiling. Most nights, when everybody else was asleep, I'd find myself wandering the house, eventually ending up in my mother's room, where I'd cuddle up to her, and only then would I finally drift off.

I can picture myself ambling across the living room in darkness.

My naked soles kiss against the hardwood floor, the only sound except for the odd creak as the house settles. The house gets more rest than I do. I walk to the windows. We have large windows, at least five feet high, that stretch, pane by pane, from one side of the room to the other. At night, my mother closes the curtains. The room is awash in black. I open the curtains, and a soft, white light descends on me like fog.

On clear nights, the stars would be bright and crisp, and I

would begin to count them as though I were counting sheep, as if doing so would make me tired. But that night, like many nights, I give up soon after I start because the number is immeasurable. I would close the curtains again, trying to shut myself off from infinity but feeling more awake and unsettled than before.

Looking back, I can understand how the endlessness of the sky overwhelmed me and how my time-travelling thoughts led me back to that place. I used to play a movie in my mind that I was on a rocket ship destined for the end of the universe, the end of space. I would try to wrap my head around the fact that I would never reach my destination no matter how long I travelled; that I would grow old and die and the ship would keep on going forever. My maternal grandmother used to tell me that she never felt older than a teenager, even when she'd reached her eighties. I know what she was talking about now; I feel as though I'm only playing an adult, when most of the time, I'm still that scared, insecure, disillusioned, goofy, desperate-for-love teenager, freaked out by the vastness of the universe.

The stars mean more to me now than they did then. These days, I don't often think about them in terms of numbers but rather in terms of stories, and this makes me feel more wonder than dread. As Wilfred Buck, affectionately known by children as "the Star Guy," says: "We originate from the stars, we are star people . . . this is where we come from . . . we are related to those stars. Once we finish doing what we come here to do, we go back up to those stars." What a beautiful concept. It's a notion I try to ingrain in my way of knowing so that the stars don't alienate me but rather call me home. I do my best to think of them as I do about Norway House or my father's trapline; I belong there, and there isn't room for fear in that belonging. After all, how can you be afraid of a place that is a part of you?

One strategy for living with anxiety is to speak louder than it can, to change the way you see yourself and the world around you. It's in the terminology of mental health. If you work on the mental component, the physical ailments that follow destructive thoughts, including fear, can be allayed. When I begin to feel small, I repeat what Buck has said. We all need mantras to get us through the day, sometimes through the hour, or just through the moment.

I carry the universe around with me.

Imagine that; what a contrast. If only I could have made that jump four decades ago, from feeling so overwhelmingly small and, by association, meaningless to being able to carry the entirety of it all in the palms of my hands. I couldn't do it when I was a young boy, and I can do it only sometimes now.

At the height of my anxiety, during my nervous breakdown, I visited my doctor. We were talking about medication versus therapy for what I was going through.

"Do I have to take medication?" I asked. "Can't I just go to a psychologist?"

This may come as a shock, but I was worried about using benzos or antidepressants. They're mind-altering drugs. I mean, I'm worried about eating dark chocolate because it could stimulate my PVCs, so of course I'd be concerned about taking strong medication like alprazolam. What I didn't get at first is that, in the state I was in, it was necessary. Whether or not I still need it today is another conversation entirely.

"David," he said, "you can't change the way you think overnight. You have to give your mind a break so it can get there."

No shit. That was years ago, and I still haven't entirely changed the way I think. I've improved in many respects, but I fall back on old habits, like googling symptoms to figure out what's wrong with me, as though I can know more from reading webMD.com for five minutes than a medical professional who has trained for years.

Let's give childhood David a pass on what he wished he'd known, and maybe adult David too, while we're at it. There's no place for judgment anywhere in the world of mental health, not towards yourself, and not towards others. I have come to learn that kindness, above all else, is the most productive thing.

The sleepless nights were the first phase of my mental health struggles, and my journey since that time will forever be entangled with those dark hours standing in front of the window, staring past the stars into space, trying to reconcile the enormity of infinity with my tiny life. To understand how a single molecule could be noteworthy in any way.

Back then I didn't connect that feeling to death, or a fear of it. Not yet. If we look at mental health using the metaphor of a seed's life cycle, you could place the knowledge of death as the germination of anxiety.

When did I eat the apple, as it were?

For children, there's an age where death doesn't resonate; it's difficult to understand that somebody is gone and that they aren't coming back. I think, in some ways, the innocence of youth insulates us from that reality.

My great-grandparents on my mom's side lived in Melita, a small town in southwest Manitoba about a three-and-a-half-hour drive from Winnipeg, just a few blocks away from my grandparents. There are several reasons why I can vividly remember visiting them, not the least of which was their pink house, the only house in the entire town painted that colour. I never knew the street address, but I didn't have to. I could see it from Summit Street, the road that led past the hospital and ended at the golf course. My great-grandmother had a lot of breakable stuff. Porcelain knick-knacks. A nightmare for young visiting kids like me. On the coffee table, she kept a full jar of mints that melted in your mouth. I think they were pink, just like the house. She was hilarious, like my grandmother. A bunch of us, the whole family, would play cards in her living room, and we'd often catch her cheating. She thought she was subtle, leaning to the side and peeking over an opponent's shoulder to see their hand, but she was painfully obvious. Still, we let her do it, and she probably won as a result, but I can't recall that to a certainty.

She had soft, smooth, warm skin, and it was pale like milk. I remember touching her hand a lot, because it felt comfortable, like a security blanket. She had curly white hair, and thick glasses. She used to feed me sandwiches.

And then she was dead.

In the middle of the night, my great-grandmother quietly got up from bed and went to the bathroom. Then she crawled back under the sheets, said goodnight to her husband, closed her eyes, and passed away.

The viewing was held at the Presbyterian church beside my grandparents' house. I'd walked by it more times than I could count, but the only time I went inside was to see my great-grandmother's body. I don't remember much about the inside of the church. What I do remember is my great-grandfather being helped up the aisle, step by step down the red carpet, to the casket that held his wife's body. Once there, he reached out and with a shaking hand touched her skin. Then he collapsed to his knees, as if praying for her return. The church was quiet, but his sobs filled the room louder than a congregation. I watched this happen curiously, and I can't say that I grasped the reaction. I'd viewed my great-grandmother's body, too. I'd touched her hand. It was cold and hard and her skin moved as if she'd been moulded with Plasticine. But I didn't think that was sad.

I sat with my family—Mom and my brothers, Grandma and Grandpa—at the reception. There were tiny sandwiches (they reminded me of the kind that my great-grandmother used to make me) and treats. I had a cup full of orange juice. While we ate, in front of a crowd of mourners, I stood up and raised my glass and yelled, "Cheers!" I don't know why I did that, but Grandma put a stop to it quickly and gently. She put her hand on my forearm and lowered my cup, shaking her head. She told me that we didn't do that at funerals. I suppose I saw a room full of people who were there for Great-Grandmother, and it seemed like a celebration,

so "Cheers!" felt appropriate. The finality of her loss didn't resonate, the fact that Grandma's mother was gone, and she wasn't
coming back.

When you're young, death seems so far away. It's far enough
away that you can hold on to the hope of immortality, because a
grandparent? They're ancient. When you're eight, the age I was
when my great-grandmother died, being seventy is unfathom-
able. When Ken, our next-door neighbour, turned forty years
old, even that age seemed one step towards the grave. Jo-Ann,
his wife, put a sign on their front yard that read "Honk! Ken's 40!"
and all day, honks crowded out all other sounds. One car after
another, as though ominously counting down the years. When I
turned forty, I instantly thought back to Ken, who's still with us,
and thought, *Shit, forty isn't that old*, but I got there faster than I
thought I would. It was bittersweet.

Death, though, was for old people. When mother gave us the
news that Great-Grandpa passed away, we were accepting of
it. Of course, we'd have preferred that he not be dead, but there
was, at the same time, something pretty about imagining him
lying in bed with his wife once more.

In the eighth grade, the possibility of death, the heaviness of it,
became all too real. It was our first class back to River Heights
Junior High after a gloriously long Christmas break. The class
was a bit rowdy—everybody was still in holiday mode—but my
classmates and I were quieted by the principal, who never really
showed his face in individual classrooms. That was weird. What's

more, his already-white face was ghostly. So pale that he was translucent. It looked as though he'd spent the night on a bender and was two seconds away from vomiting in the army-green metal garbage bin on the floor beside Mr. Morrisseau's desk. He asked for the class's attention, and was given it; he then stood in silence for a moment, gathering himself, before explaining what had happened. Over Christmas break, Patrick Brown, one of the most popular kids in the class, was in the back seat of his family car, on the highway, when a backhoe reversed onto the road and a collision followed. Patrick and his entire family were killed instantly. The principal told us that counselling was available if we needed it. A couple of Patrick's closer friends left class immediately; I remember one of them had lost all the colour in his face—just like our principal—as he slung his backpack over his shoulder and walked across the room, out the door.

I didn't have many friends in junior high school. Sure, I was bullied a little bit. In the eighth grade, I hadn't lost my baby fat yet, hadn't sprouted, so I was overweight. I had zero self-confidence and didn't really know how to talk to other kids, so I didn't do it often. I'd tried out for the basketball team and was cut, which didn't help with the whole confidence thing. And, of course, as I wrote about in my first memoir, *Black Water*, I was dealing with significant identity issues; I didn't like being Indigenous and didn't think other people would like me if they knew the truth. I guess I spent more time hiding my identity than trusting that most kids wouldn't have treated me any different if they knew I was Cree. Patrick had been nice to everybody. He had a close group of friends, but if you asked most people in the class, they would've told you that they were friends of his, too. He was always in a good mood. I never saw him grumpy, or sad. He made this contraption out of a pen and likely an entire roll of masking tape. It looked like a mace, only without the metal and the spikes. He called it his Happy Fun Ball. If he hit you with it, you had to be happy. One of my classmates, a girl, drew a picture of Patrick with his Happy Fun Ball after his death. I don't know what happened to it. I'd like to think somebody kept it, that it's out there somewhere. I think Patrick would've liked the thought of that.

That death changed everything for me. Kids think they're invincible, that they're immortal. Consequently, they do the stupidest things. There's not typically a thought process that includes the possibility of death, because kids don't die. But then, one of us did, which meant we all could.

Those nights I spent wandering through the house, those feelings of insignificance, of being a molecule against the vastness of eternity, my attempts to comprehend the concept of forever—at some point in my teenage years, they turned inward. I wasn't only obsessed with what forever was. Now I was obsessed with my relationship with eternity, due to a fragile mortality. I thought I had years. I thought I had decades. Maybe I did, maybe I didn't. I could tumble into forever at any moment. I could get into a car accident on the highway. I could get cancer. I replayed moments of my life where I'd almost died, and wondered why I hadn't.

I stopped wandering the house. I stopped staring out the window, at the stars, and then, beyond them. I stopped feeling as if I were a molecule. Instead, I took to pressing my face into a pillow and screaming at the unfairness of it all, at life being a tease. You don't give somebody something, something as big as existence, only to take it away so quickly. It makes *existence* feel like a molecule, not just you. Because when you think about it, within a hundred years, every single person on this earth, except for a handful of lucky ones who'll reach triple digits and have to eat soup through a straw, will be dead. I don't know if that's comforting or horrifying. I really don't. All I know is that I didn't want it to happen to me. I wanted to be the only person in the history of the world to never die, so that I would never be thrust into a ceaseless black. Or, at the very least, I wanted to be one of those old dudes in the Bible who lived to be seven hundred. Seven hundred was a long time. Seven hundred was acceptably close to eternity, especially for a kid.

At least I was healthy. It lowered my chances of dying young. And during my formative years, there wasn't a history of early deaths or serious illnesses in my family to worry about. Trust me, if there were, I would've worried about them. Nana, my grandmother on my dad's side, died from some kind of pulmonary issue, which was common for First Nations people. I mean, the number of us who've died of tuberculosis is overwhelming, but I didn't live in conditions that made TB a likelihood. My uncle died from HIV/AIDS, and while I did worry I had HIV once, it wasn't likely. I didn't share needles or anything like that, and I was a virgin forever. There was no history of cancer, and old age—what Great-Grandmother died of—well, you can't catch something like that. Eventually, it catches you, but if you're careful, as I increasingly became, you can be elusive.

I didn't ever worry about my heart either. Never noticed it, except at odd times, late at night, close to sleeping but not quite dreaming. There's no history, that I'm aware of, of heart disease. My grandmother on Mom's side may have died from heart failure, but she was also, no matter how young she told me she felt in her mind, an old woman. Eventually, for everybody, the heart will fail.

Once, when I lay with my head on the pillow, my ear pressed against fabric, I heard footsteps. It sounded as though somebody were walking through the snow. I pictured somebody doing just that, one step after the other. After this imaginary person had been walking for quite some time, through an endless field of snow, I realized the sound was my heart, beating in perfect rhythm.

TWO
CONFIRMATION BIAS

After germination, a plant begins to grow.

Under the right conditions, or, in this case, the wrong conditions, the seed of anxiety starts to take on a life of its own. There's a catalyst for this evolution, and if you don't know what it is, addressing your mental health challenges becomes a near-insurmountable task. Close your eyes for a moment and pretend you're in a kayak on the river. It's a peaceful day. The swift water urges you forward, but at the same time, there is an undeniable calmness. You can see the reflection of the surrounding trees on the surface of the river, the cotton-ball clouds wandering past you overhead, and the sun. Each time your paddle breaches the surface, it throws out capillary waves, but you leave them behind in favour of nature's serenity. You don't have sandals on; you left them by the water's edge. You start to feel water pooling around your naked feet and don't think much of it at first, because you're in the water, you're throwing water into the air with the movement of your paddles, so you're bound to get wet. But then the water begins to fill the canoe faster, and soon your entire foot is submerged, then your calves, then your knees, then your thighs. Smartly, you brought a small bucket, and you bail.

This helps to keep the water at bay, and prevents you from sinking; however, you can't paddle anymore, so now you're just drifting away, going wherever the current brings you, completely out of control and forever preoccupied with the water that keeps coming, no matter how much you throw over the side. You have to know where the leak is. Once you know where it is, where the flooding originated, you can plug it, and when you plug it, you can start paddling again. You'll be in control once more. If you leave it, that leak, that little crack, is going to keep pouring water, and before you know it, you'll be going under. And that current? It's strong.

There was more than the one thing that kick-started my anxiety, and everything that came with it—obsessive-compulsive disorder, depression, panic, hypochondriasis. I keep thinking of another analogy, as I consider the genesis of my ongoing fight against mental health issues. I picture an avalanche. There is not one thing, I don't think, that starts an avalanche. It is not simply the weight or movement of a skier that causes a large area of snow to dislodge and tumble down a mountainside. The skier would be the trigger, I suppose, but for the skier to start things off, there must be some sort of instability that already exists. I googled (I am allowed to google things that are not symptoms I think I am experiencing) "how does an avalanche start" and was told that avalanches are caused by four factors: a steep slope, snow cover, a weak layer in the snow cover, and a trigger. I'm not going to force a conversation that enlists all four factors, but I will say that the term *weak layer* keeps repeating in my mind. That speaks to fragility, and I do feel as though a fragility is likely present in order for the trigger to cause the avalanche that is anxiety.

For me, it was more than a thick fear of death and the vast oblivion that followed, although, to be fair, those are the two biggest contributing factors. It was, as I've written and spoken of before, my struggles with identity, with not feeling comfortable in my own skin, as a Cree person. When you don't understand yourself, when you form negative opinions of yourself, when you don't *want* to be yourself, it's not healthy. Over the years, I've worked hard on myself from an identity perspective, and I've come to the point where I feel strong and proud as a Cree man, but it wasn't always that way. I used to be breakable, and, in turn, this state of being contributed to the fact that I broke. These factors left me vulnerable (that weak layer), and my little plant of anxiety grew when I met with new fears and worries.

My grandfather died too early, in his seventies. But it wasn't only that he died; it was how he died—from ALS, or amyotrophic lateral sclerosis, a rare neurological disease. After learning about his illness, and following his death, even right up until this moment in time, as I sit at my dining room table writing these words, every little muscle twitch is like a jump scare that leaves me having to catch my breath. Talk about fragility. I could go on and on (and on and on), listing everything that laid the very shaky foundation of my avalanche, but in the interest of brevity, let's just say that many things manufactured conditions that allowed the trigger to do its work. Your conditions and trigger are likely different, but it's worth figuring them out.

*

After high school, I wanted to stay involved with the game of basketball, and I agreed to coach the junior varsity boys' team at Kelvin High School with my friend Chris. Chris was the head coach, and I was a great cheerleader for the kids. Chris and I liked to challenge our players in practice. Because we were young, fresh out of high school ourselves, we often scrimmaged with them.

I don't remember when it happened, just that it happened. We were in the middle of a scrimmage when I took a step towards the basket and, as if a switch had been flicked, my heart started to jackhammer. It went from a normal rhythm for a young guy in good shape in the middle of a high-intensity workout to beating over two hundred times per minute. And it wasn't only that it was beating too fast; it felt wrong. I stopped playing instantly, didn't say anything to Chris or our players, walked to the sideline, and lay down on a bench. I didn't know what was going on, only that whatever it was, it wasn't normal. I put my hand on my chest and could feel my heart sprinting. I looked at my shirt, and it was vibrating. It wasn't long before everybody noticed. They came to check on me to see what was up, and I told them I just needed to rest for a second. I wasn't worried, which, given my history, is odd. But at that point in my life, my brain didn't automatically go to the worst-case scenario when it came to health concerns. I lay there until I felt one hard beat, like a reset, and my heart started beating normally again. As soon as it did, I told the guys that I was good to go, got up, and started playing again.

When I think back on that first experience with an irregular heartbeat, I long for that sort of rational reaction. I felt what was happening (it would've been impossible to ignore), but I knew that it was highly unlikely I was having a heart attack, as I wasn't even twenty at the time, so I didn't freak out or call an ambulance, and after things felt normal again, I went about my day. It wasn't that I thought a normal thing had happened. It was just that it didn't seem like a big deal; my heart had never done that before, I didn't think it would happen again, and I had things to do. This is not to say that I considered it something I should ignore. I told Mom what had happened, and we made an appointment so that I could ask my doctor about it. He would know more than I would. All I knew was that my heart beat super-fast for a minute, and then started beating normally again. It came out of nowhere, and it ended out of nowhere. I suppose it's a good thing that, back then, there was no internet. If there had been, I might have googled the abnormal heart rhythm, and the results would've worried me.

Not long after that first episode (I took to calling them episodes as they became more frequent, and I got used to having them), I went to my doctor's appointment. I told him what had happened. He assured me that it *was* normal, which I didn't quite believe, but he was the doctor, and I had no medical training. He explained that I'd grown tall quickly, and a lot of things were still trying to catch up, including my heart. Sure, I'd gotten tall several years ago, between grade eight and nine, but whatever. Fine. At some point, my systems would level out, and my heart wouldn't go bonkers like that anymore. Until then, the solution was simple. I had to watch my caffeine intake, because things like coffee or Coke (the soda, not the drug, although he did tell me that recreational drugs wouldn't be smart) might set off my heart. That was it. When I left the doctor's office, I left any worry or thought about my heart behind. The brief one-minute episode didn't get another moment of time in my brain until it happened again. And again. And again. Until it had happened too many times to count. And although the first time my heart went haywire was while playing basketball, which made it somewhat understandable, exercise didn't seem to be the catalyst.

My heart never went into hyperdrive when lying in bed doing nothing, but there were times when it didn't take much to touch it off. Once, in the middle of the day, before I stopped eating meat, I was minding my own business, eating a sausage. As soon as I swallowed, there it went. Come to think of it, an early indication of my anxiety stemmed from that moment, because after that incident, I'm relatively certain I didn't eat sausage as much as I did before. Sometimes when I moved a certain way my heart didn't agree, and it would start to beat rapidly in protest. I would bend down to tie my shoes while out walking, and there it would go. Or, although it never kicked in when I was sedentary, more than a few times getting up too quickly after sitting for a while was enough to set it off. Still, most of my episodes were caused by a physical stressor. I got into a multi-vehicle accident in downtown Winnipeg, and as soon as the car behind me rammed into my rear bumper, my heart let me know it didn't appreciate the impact. It raced like crazy, as if it were trying to get away. Basketball continued to be a frequent culprit, most often causing my irregular heartbeat when I landed after jumping. Once it happened right after the jump ball at the start of a game, and I had to sub myself off immediately. I sat on the bench and waited for it to reset, and when it did, I subbed back in and played the game as if nothing at all had happened.

That was how it went for about five years. Almost like clockwork, which was ironic considering my heart's irregularity, I could count on having an episode at least once a month. Due to their frequency, I practised strategies to quell the arrhythmia. I would splash ice-cold water onto my face. I would bear down as if I had to take a shit. I would jump up and down, because that's what jolted it into beating so fast, so why wouldn't it do the opposite as well? I would rub one of my carotid arteries. Sometimes one of those procedures would do the trick; other times my heart settled down on its own terms, in its own time.

What I was thankful for, if there were things to be thankful for, in having a recurring irregular heartbeat, was that no matter what caused the episode, it never lasted too long. Sure, in the heat of the moment, it felt as if it lasted an hour, but it was really only a minute or two, and never more than that. What I was not thankful for was that as time moved on, my doctor kept repeating that it was just growing pains, that it would resolve itself. Just give it a little more time. I mean, at twenty-four years of age, exactly when was I going to "grow out of it"? Something was wrong, and I knew it, even if nobody else did. The problem was that nobody was ever able to catch it on an ECG. My doctor, despite his belief that it was natural, set up one or two electrocardiograms, but those tests were useless unless my heart happened to sprint while hooked up to all the wires.

And then it happened. It turned out to be one of the scariest nights of my life, and one of the most necessary.

I started playing ultimate frisbee in the nineties, when the sport was still young in Manitoba. My job, for the first few years I played, was to run as fast as I could towards the end zone and catch discs that were thrown in my general direction. Unsurprisingly, I had a heart episode or two while playing, but just like every other time, they didn't last very long, and as luck would have it, there was a cardiologist on our team, so that made me feel comfortable. One night in the early 2000s, on a lower-division team with my friend Dan (but without the cardiologist), at Kildonan Park, we played an epic game that lasted way longer than it should have. Back then, the rules were that the first team to reach 15 won, but you had to win by two. So, if the score was 15–14, you had to get to 16 to win the game. This particular match went all the way into the 20s before we eventually lost. I played most of the marathon game, and when it was over, I was tired. Even still, I made it through alright. My heart had behaved. I wasn't even thinking about it. I never did unless it started to beat recklessly. I thought my doctor was wrong, but I never freaked out when it went funny, because it always resolved, either on its own or with a little help.

I was taking off my cleats and putting on my sandals as the sunset began to throw warm colours across the sky like spilled paint when it happened. I felt the click in my chest that always preceded my arrhythmia, and sure enough, it kicked into high gear. I didn't say anything. I'd gotten used to waiting it out. Even though it was an uncomfortable feeling, it was fleeting. I stopped chatting with Dan in favour of incorporating some of my strategies, but I planned on keeping up the conversation as soon as my heart clicked back into its normal rhythm. I poured some water into my hands and splashed it on my face. That didn't work. I bore down as if I had to go to the bathroom. My heart kept racing. I rubbed my carotid artery with no luck. Okay. No problem. The strategies didn't *always* work. I'd have to wait for that bump in my chest to signal that my heart had slowed its pace. But minutes later, it was still racing, beating over two hundred times per minute, even though the game had ended half an hour ago. That's when, for the first time, I started to worry.

"I think I have to go to the hospital," I said to Dan.

It was an about-face from the conversation we'd just been having about the game. It would've come as a shock to Dan, because to him, I wouldn't have looked like anything was going on; I guess even back then I could hide an internal struggle well. At most, I would have looked slightly pale, but the only person who's consistently been able to tell when something's wrong with me is Jill. I'm not certain Dan knew about my ongoing heart issue, but after telling him what was happening, we were in his car within a couple of minutes, driving away from Kildonan Park, on the way to Seven Oaks General Hospital.

Even pre-pandemic, emergency room wait times left a lot to be desired. Before I describe my experience, I'm going to address the elephant in the room about health care and being Indigenous. I am Cree. But when you look at me, I don't look like the stereotypical Indigenous person, whatever that means. Yes, there are times when I'm followed around a store when I'm dressed in ripped jeans and a hooded sweatshirt; no matter how you dress you cannot remove your brown skin. But for the most part, I'm left alone. And in hospitals, I'm not treated differently. Is this because I don't sound like I'm from the rez? I don't have long, braided hair? I have moccasins but typically just wear them around the house. I live in Westwood, an upper-class neighbourhood in Winnipeg. This is a different sort of story, but the truth is, if you're Indigenous and enter a hospital, you can have a serious concern about getting the same quality of care as others. I don't fit into the preconception that exists for what it means to be, as the news used to say, "Aboriginal in appearance." But a lot of us don't conform to any of the expectations others have of us. For those of us that do, attending an emergency room in the city can add an extra stressor to an already stressful situation. It's impossible not to think of Brian Sinclair, who, in September 2008, attended Winnipeg's Health Sciences Centre and waited for thirty-four hours to receive medical attention. He died while waiting. He'd been dead in the waiting room for so long that by the time medical staff attended to him, he'd developed rigor mortis. A story like this hits close to home for my family. A month earlier, in August 2008, my auntie Olive waited several hours in the emergency room for treatment at the same hospital; she'd developed an infection after undergoing gallbladder surgery. She died two days later. In a lawsuit against the Winnipeg Regional Health Authority, the family contended that my auntie's death could've been avoided if she'd been treated immediately after arriving at the hospital via ambulance.

While the unnecessary deaths of Indigenous people within the health-care system are not rare, I have to acknowledge that there are far more good people working in health care than there are bad, or ignorant. I mean, there are bad people everywhere, in every industry and system in this country. But there are, I'd like to think, far more good people—I get that hope from working so much with teachers and librarians and kids.

On that day—the day when my heart wouldn't stop racing its familiar, irregular rhythm—I was lucky to have good nurses and doctors looking after me, and also lucky that when it comes to matters of the heart, medical professionals don't fuck around. When Dan and I pulled up to Seven Oaks General Hospital, I didn't know what to expect. I'd been to the ER enough times, for myself or with one of my kids, that I had no idea how long I'd have to wait. Back then, there was no "emergency department wait time" website, so we just picked the closest hospital and hoped it wasn't too crowded. When we walked inside, we saw that the waiting room was full. I started to imagine sitting on one of those uncomfortable chairs with my heart pounding for hours, but it didn't play out that way. As soon as the triage nurse took my pulse, I was brought right in and given a bed. Dan stayed behind in the waiting room and got on the phone to tell my wife the situation.

I didn't like what was happening. I hated it when I had an episode. Up until that night, I'd not worried about my heart; it was an annoyance I had to wait out, until it kicked back into a normal rhythm. It was annoying, too, that not only did my doctor not know what caused it, but he also didn't know what was going on when it started to thump. The thing with heart problems is that you have to catch them in action in order to assess them. Even though I'd been living with this problem for years at that point, it had never been caught on an ECG, as I said, so it was only a feeling I'd reported, and nothing quantifiable. My irregular, sprinting heart was Snuffleupagus. But, as I lay there on a hard bed, covered with heated blankets and hooked up to a bunch of leads, they finally got it documented on a long, thin strip of paper with lines that looked like a mountain range. I was starting to panic, given how long my heart had been racing, but oddly, I was also relieved. *Finally*, they'd see what I'd been complaining about. It wasn't growing pains. Growing pains kept you up at night with a sore leg; you didn't wind up at a hospital from them. I kept picturing my doctor seeing the ECG report and me saying, "I told you so!"

But first, there was the small matter of saving my life.

The emergency room doctor told me that normally what was happening wasn't life-threatening, except for when it went on for a long period of time. By then, my heart had been sprinting for almost an hour, and the benign nature of my condition was, to me at least, quickly becoming a matter of grave concern.

We tried the regular methods, the ones I'd come to know well. The doctor rubbed my carotid artery (one of them at a time, not both, even though both seemed appropriate as I grew more desperate); I splashed my face with ice water; I bore down (I bore down so hard and so desperately that night I'm still surprised I didn't shit myself). But none of it worked. The next step was drugs. An IV was already in my arm, so I was given calcium channel blockers with an assurance from the doctor that the intervention would likely help; calcium channel blockers were usually effective. After a few minutes, though, nothing had changed. After the first round of medicine, I was given beta blockers, which essentially do the same thing as calcium channel blockers. Both are used for similar problems; the calcium channel blockers inhibit the flow of calcium, while beta blockers directly block beta receptors from being activated (I have no idea what any of that means). I received two rounds of beta blockers, and my heart didn't slow.

Things were getting real. I could feel it, and I could hear and see it in the doctor's tone of voice and body language. Don't get me wrong: he was great. He stayed calm, and, in turn, I kept as calm as possible. But there are some things you can't hide, and he was growing concerned. He stood at my bedside, looking down on me as I tried to ignore my chest vibrating through the heated blankets, long since grown cold. He told me that we could wait it out, and hope that my heart would start beating normally again, but that didn't feel like a viable option to me; there was something inside me that knew my heart wasn't going to "click" back on its own. If it were going to do that, it would've done it by then. A heart episode had never gone on this long before. Not even close. As soon as the doctor gave me that "hurry up and wait" option, I knew it wasn't possible for me. My heart rate was astronomical, my blood pressure was totally fucked, and I'd started to feel dizzy and light-headed. The doctor then repeated to me what he'd told the nurse earlier.

"The longer this goes on, the more dangerous it gets."

Their plan was to reboot my heart. Reboot my heart?

"What does that mean?" I asked.

He explained that they would stop it and then restart it. They'd use a defibrillator to conduct a procedure called electrical cardioversion.

"Is that dangerous?" I asked. "I mean, what if you stop it and you can't restart it."

"We've never had that happen before," he assured me.

Here's the thing.

When you have anxiety, even if it's not full-blown anxiety, you pick apart statements that are meant to be encouraging, that should instill confidence. A regular person who doesn't live with anxiety would hear that statement—"We've never had that happen before"—and think to themselves, *Phew. It's never happened before. I'm in*, or something to that effect. An anxiety sufferer hears that statement and thinks, *They've never had that happen before, which means it's possible for it to happen. What the doctor really means is that it hasn't happened* yet. Still, despite my trepidation, I didn't see another choice; it was the lesser of two evils. I could either let my heart race and hope that it slowed down of its own volition, and if it didn't, possibly go into cardiac arrest, or I could get cardioverted, have my heart stopped and then restarted, which was, according to the medical professional, a sure-fire solution. Weighing the two choices—one where it was possible I'd go into cardiac arrest if I did nothing, the other where it was very likely I'd be okay—I decided on the electrical cardioversion.

"Is it going to hurt?" I asked.

The good thing about this choice was that I wouldn't be aware of anything. My chest would be sore afterwards, but during and immediately after it would hurt worse getting bit by a mosquito. Why? The doctor said that he would give me a drug prior to the cardioversion that would wipe my memory of the whole affair, even though I'd be completely lucid. I would be awake, but when the medicine wore off, I wouldn't remember about an hour of my life.

"That sounds a lot like truth serum," I said.

It wasn't far off. I would be disinhibited, and as a result, unable to lie. I thought that was the only cool thing that was going to happen to me. Minutes later, with Jill on the way and Dan in the waiting room, only able to see my feet from his vantage point, the nurse stuck a needle into my IV and gave me the truth serum (I'm calling it that; I don't know what it was called for real). I can't say that I had to dramatically count down from ten, but at some point in the next several seconds I jumped forward approximately sixty minutes in time, in a snap. An hour lost.

I've only learned about what happened during those sixty minutes from second-hand accounts, my sources being the nurse, Dan, and my wife. The only souvenir I got from that hour was a sore chest, just as the doctor had warned me of, which got even sorer the next day. But I suppose that's what happens when you get the paddles not once, but twice. Dan told me that he saw me being cardioverted. He was looking at my feet, which, given my height, were sticking out from underneath the thin hospital blankets (I think they're heated because they're so thin). He saw my feet lift off the bed in a sudden movement, and then relax. Moments later, my feet rose a second time, and that was that. After the second shock, my heart was steered into a normal rhythm, and I was out of the woods, whatever type of forest I'd found myself in. When Jill arrived at the hospital, she explained that my mother was home watching our baby (we only had Emily at the time); I asked her why my mother hadn't come and she, Jill, had. Jill was a bit annoyed and hurt by what I'd said, and that was understandable. (It wasn't my fault! It was the truth serum—though it's true that I've always been a momma's boy, especially when I was younger, and Dad wasn't living with us.) What I didn't articulate then, and probably should have, is that Jill's been as much of an anchor in my life. She's always made me feel safe, not just by her presence, but in her refusal to play into my unsubstantiated worries. She'll listen to them, but she won't get played by them like I do.

That's another thing. If you do live with anxiety, panic, or depression, you need an anchor—somebody who can walk the very delicate line of telling it like it is while being sensitive to the reality of your mental health battle. Somebody who understands that you don't want to feel the way you do and you don't want your brain to think the way it does, but often, no matter how hard you try, and even though you are aware of what you're doing and why you're feeling the way you are, you can't help it. You need somebody who's able to look you in the eyes and tell you, directly, that while you most certainly do have a headache, it's very likely not a malignant brain tumour. You will live, whether you take an Advil or not. I've got that anchor in my life in Jill, but it doesn't have to be your spouse. It can be a friend, a family member, an accountability partner, a therapist—even somebody who's going through what you're going through. I've been living with mental health issues for so long that I've gotten good at providing support and advice to others who are living with similar barriers. I can give great advice if you're living with GAD, depression, health anxiety, or OCD. It comes from experience and from working with great therapists and specialized psychiatrists. What I suck at is taking my own advice, because there's always that monster on my shoulder, talking in my ear, discounting everything I think I know in favour of its lies. I'm working on it. But the fact remains: You need the rational to counteract the irrationality of it all. You need a different voice on your shoulder.

But back to the heart.

After years of trying to catch my irregular heart doing its thing, of having to provide best-guess scenarios because there was no evidence to support any real diagnosis, we finally got it on paper. That was a frightening incident, there are no two ways around it, but it was a crucial incident, and I've come to appreciate that. When my doctor got the emergency report from Seven Oaks General Hospital, the wheels were set in motion. The. Very. Slow. Wheels. Of. Non-urgent. Medical. Care. In. Canada. There are a lot of great things about free health care; one of the not-so-great things is that if you're not suffering from a life-threatening ailment, you've got to wait. My heart condition was concerning, but it was, at the moment at least, not going to kill me. And so, my doctor ordered a battery of tests, but cautioned that it would be a long while until I got them all done and we had a confirmed diagnosis. There was no treatment until that time. I had to keep doing what I'd been doing: deal with it when I had an episode and, for me at least, hope that I didn't have to go to the emergency room again.

"How long will I have to wait?" I asked.

My doctor's best guess was two years. Part of me thought, *That's okay, I've already been living with this for a long time, what's another two years?* The other part of me thought, *Jesus, I could've been getting tests done in the late nineties.* I was impatient, and luckily, so were my parents. Especially Mom. Mom, like so many other mothers out there, goes full-on Momma Bear when she has to. She's the kindest, sweetest person, but if you mess with her kids, you are done. When it came to the prospect of waiting two years to get all the tests done on my heart, my mother was having none of it. A neighbour of ours had gone to the Mayo Clinic in Rochester, Minnesota, for a different ailment and got done in days what would have taken years in Canada. Mom decided, along with Dad, that that was exactly what we were going to do. Our family doctor was asked to refer us to the Mayo Clinic. He did, and within a month or two, Mom and I were on a plane to Minnesota to see a cardiologist, with Mom and Dad prepared to pay whatever it cost for a diagnosis.

I spent two days at the Mayo Clinic, and during that time, received several tests, alongside an assessment of the ECG and emergency room report from Seven Oaks General Hospital. When the tests were complete, no more than forty-eight hours after I'd stepped into the hospital, I was given the diagnosis I'd been waiting for. I had SVT, or supraventricular tachycardia. Straight from the Mayo Clinic's website, SVT is a fast and erratic heartbeat that affects the upper chambers. Your average, every-day heart (I'm paraphrasing all of this) beats about 60 to 100 times per minute. During an episode of SVT, the heart beats from 150 to 220 times per minute. Most people don't need interventions or treatment, which is bewildering to me. Back then, and some-times even now, I couldn't imagine being okay living with it, not knowing when it was going to happen, and waiting it out when it did. Or getting shocked in the chest with paddles. For other people, lifestyle changes or medical interventions may control or even eliminate the problem. Elimination sounded good to me. I wanted to make my heart issue like a failed contestant on *Survivor*. As soon as I heard that my irregular heart could be corrected, there was no decision. Why would I live with it when it could be gone from my life entirely?

The folks at the Mayo Clinic were ready to do the procedure on the spot, right then. Mom was ready to pay for it, too, and it wasn't cheap. I don't have the numbers in front of me, but I re-call the cost was going to double the bill that had already been accrued in the two days we'd been at the hospital. While I was anxious to fix my heart, I was not anxious to potentially send my parents into a huge amount of debt. I told Mom that I could wait to get the procedure done in Canada. I mean, I'd already lived with my heart condition for years, what was a few extra months? The doctor, in the meantime, wrote me a prescription for beta blockers, which would mostly eliminate the episodes of SVT I had been enduring, and who knew? If the medicine worked well,

I might find that staying on them, and avoiding heart surgery (it was non-invasive, but there were still risks involved), was best. The victory of our trip down to Rochester was that we finally knew what was wrong with my heart, and we knew what we could do to fix it. That was all I'd ever wanted. I had been confident something was not right with my heart, and I'd needed to know what was wrong. After all those years, going back to that first episode in the basketball gym in the late nineties, I felt vindicated.

Within two days, back on Canadian soil, I took my first pill to see how effective the beta blockers would be.

Here's another thing about anxiety. One of many things about anxiety. I have found, through experience and anecdotal evidence, that the thought processes for those who live with mental health issues are similar. I'm sure that somebody reading this, at some point in this book, will think to themselves, *That's me. I've felt that way, too.* And in the end, that's what this is all about. I want you to see yourself in my story, because I guarantee you that I can see myself in yours. That's why we share, and that's how we work towards healing.

I have an aversion to medication. That's ironic to say, because currently, I'm taking three types of medication—alprazolam, bupropion, and metoprolol—but starting to take each one of them, believe me, was a struggle. It was like pulling teeth. I'm naming my medications because normalizing mental health also includes normalizing the medicine we take to help live with whatever mental health obstacles we have in front of us. Despite what Tom Cruise might've said in the past (love his movies, by the way), medication, when prescribed and used properly, can save lives. I know. It helped save mine.

But even though medication has helped me a great deal, it's frightening to start taking it. I know what the medication is supposed to do for me (with alprazolam, for example, it's going to prevent the worry in my brain from affecting my body to the degree that it does; with metoprolol, it'll lower my blood pressure and heart rate so that my PVCs aren't as pronounced, and thus aren't as disruptive), but I cannot prevent myself from reading about the side effects, and as soon as I do, I'm playing a movie in my head about all the bad things that could happen to me. Am I going to be one of the 10 percent of people who experience respiratory difficulties? Blurred vision? Nausea? Worse yet, what if I have an epileptic seizure? I remember taking bupropion for the first time, placing it on my tongue, and then drinking a sip of water to feel it slide down my throat. I briefly considered making myself vomit before the coating of the pill could dissolve. I was very dramatic about the whole process; I'd avoided taking it for days. There's just so much scary shit on Google, for everything, but especially for medication side effects. The best rule of thumb is to trust the doctor, trust the pharmacist, trust the psychiatrist. They've considered the dangers, the mild side effects, and they've decided that those often-small risks are far outweighed by the benefits. Yes, for anxiety, there are other things you can do to manage it in your life, and medication doesn't negate that. But sometimes a little white pill helps. It doesn't have to be forever, but until you're ready to fully stand on your own two feet, there's no shame in having a small crutch.

It's okay.

Those are two more vital words. I find myself repeating them in my mind even when I'm at my worst. You know the old adage that tells us, to quote Harvey Dent from *The Dark Knight* (because I'm a huge nerd), "The night is darkest just before the dawn"? I try to remember that in those times where I am certain that I will never feel better, that this is my lot in life, and how am I going to make it if that's the case? I try to remember that it's going to be okay. And the great thing about that is there are many different iterations of being okay, of the application of the phrase, "It's okay."

If your mental health is so bad that you can't get out of bed. If you cannot think to do anything other than lie there, and you're not even sure you can make it across the hallway and into the bathroom. If going to work seems like a Herculean task, like climbing Mount Everest, and the only way you can summon the strength to make it through the eight excruciating hours is that you know at the end of it you can go home and get back into bed where it's safe. If you are at rock bottom, and so deep down in a pit that you are convinced you will never find your way out of it. I want to tell you that *it will be okay*. Maybe not today. Maybe not tomorrow. But it will be okay. Your job is to make it through that day, that tomorrow, until the pit feels a bit shallower, and climbing out of it seems like a possibility. And do you know what else? Nobody really understands anxiety or struggles with mental health unless they have experienced it. Some people may be in the shit, and they don't want to admit it, or they may not be ready to talk about it, and that requires kindness above all else. I wouldn't wish what I've felt, what I still feel some days, on my worst enemy. I'd rather sit here and ask you to break both my arms and legs than feel what I feel. When I watch other people living their lives, I wonder what it would be like to feel like them, to feel normal. But first, I don't know what they're feeling. And second, just because I don't feel well doesn't mean I have to think less of myself, or be angry at myself for not being better, for not being able to go for a hike with my kids when I know they want their father to hang out with them. I ought to strive to get there so I can do those things, so I have the tools to be at that point in my journey, but for right now, for tomorrow, it's okay to not be okay. It really is.

If you make that mantra speak loudly into your being, it will, more and more, quiet the words from all those little monsters.

I stayed on the beta blockers for a year. They did the trick. Once I took the first pill, I never suffered through another episode again. In fact, since the day I started the medication, I've not had SVT once. That's about twenty years now. There have been trade-offs for the elimination of one heart issue, but I'll get to that later. And I would say that I was thrilled to be able to do things again without having to consider, or wonder, whether my heart would start to race. I would say that I was thrilled to play basketball and not have it in the back of my mind that if I jumped and landed the wrong way, my heart would start beating over two hundred times per minute. I would say that I was thrilled to be able to eat any food I wanted and have no concern that maybe a forkful of sausage would set my ol' ticker off. I would say that I was thrilled, but I was not. Objectively, I understood that I was happy about finally having a solution for the SVT. The thing was, I couldn't make myself *feel* happy about it. As a matter of fact, I couldn't feel much of anything. I don't know whether numbness was related to the medication I was on; I can't remember the type of beta blocker I was taking then. Not numbness in the way that sometimes you wake up and you can't feel your arm. Rather, numbness to emotion. Any emotion. I've often described this period of my life as a flatline. I could not feel happy. I could not feel sad. I was so in the middle that if you'd put a level on my emotions that little bubble would have been dead centre. And it was scary. What was more concerning was that Jill was concerned.

If Jill was concerned, there was a real cause for concern.

This was a precursor to depression. Depression isn't simply feeling sad. I would say that it is feeling empty. It is feeling stuck in a void, and you don't care that you're stuck, and you don't care to find a way out. Eventually, you are not stuck in the void, you *are* the void.

About six months into taking beta blockers, it was becoming clearer and clearer that staying on the medication was not tenable for me. I would much rather have had to deal with the odd rapid heartbeat than to feel nothing at all and go through life like a zombie. That's what I, and others, called me back then: a zombie. The good thing was, I didn't need to go back to the way things were. All I had to do was stick it out for another few months and set the wheels in motion for a procedure that was called an electrophysiology study (EPS) and catheter ablation. By all accounts, according to the doctors I'd spoken with, the EPS and subsequent ablation would cure me of the SVT permanently. In very rare cases, there would be a recurrence of the SVT, years after the procedure, but then you just had to have a second procedure. I kind of wished, at times, that I'd taken Mom up on her offer to just get the damn ablation done at the Mayo Clinic, but being a zombie for a little while longer beat paying tens of thousands of dollars. We like free things here in Winnipeg.

I went about my life for about six months, or maybe it's more accurate to say my imitation of life. The positive was that when you're in a daze, when you're covered in a thick fog that follows you around like dust follows Pig-Pen, time tends to go by quickly. It's kind of like when you have a dreamless sleep. You close your eyes and when you open them it feels as if you just blinked, but really, you slept for eight hours. Before I knew it, I was on a plane to London, Ontario, where the procedure was most commonly done.

At the hospital, I was given the option to be put under, or sedated. The doctor told me that being sedated was more beneficial; because I'd be lucid, I'd be able to articulate some of the symptoms when they induced a rapid heartbeat with the study. They would run four catheters through my veins, into my heart, and from there, shoot electric impulses, mapping the conduction. Science is cool, but as cool as it is, I was not willing to help the process. There was a minuscule risk of death (below 1 percent) and an overwhelming chance of success (up to 98 percent), but I opted to be put under so that if I died during the procedure (which my brain considered to be more likely), I wouldn't know it.

Suddenly, I was a child again, roaming the hallways of my house, stopping by the large living room window, peering beyond the stars. I closed my eyes and was cloaked in oblivion. While I was asleep, the doctors ran their study. Once they discovered the problem (I had an extra node that was confusing my heart and sending it into an abnormal rhythm), they strapped a metal sheet to my back and ran another catheter into my heart, designed to shoot radio waves off the metal sheet and heat it up. The catheter burned the extra node and, ostensibly, cured me.

I woke up in recovery and was told that the procedure had been (mostly) a success. The only issue was that the extra node in my heart was very close to the regular node, which meant if they burned all of it, they risked burning both nodes. That would've left me with no nodes, and in need of a pacemaker. I wasn't too keen on having a pacemaker, and so I was perfectly happy to accept that the procedure had *mostly* been successful. At worst, I might have to come back in the future to have a follow-up procedure, if the SVT reoccurred. I spent a few hours in the hospital bed with Mom and Dad at my side, and then left before supper with nothing but a bottle of aspirin that I used for a couple of weeks to avoid clotting. Before leaving the hospital, however, I had an experience that gave me one last clear memory of London.

I was lying in bed, minding my own business, feeling hopeful about the future. And why wouldn't I? I didn't have to take beta blockers any longer, which meant that I wasn't going to be a zombie. I could already tell the difference. I was happy that the procedure was over, and that my heart was fixed. I was happy, and I was able to feel happy. When I got back to the city, after a brief period to allow my body to heal, I'd be able to play sports without worry. There would be no thought of, *If I jump to block this shot, maybe when I land my heart will start going haywire.* My mind would always go there in the split second before somebody shot, as I prepared to jump and get my hand in front of the ball. My brain goes a mile a minute; that's partly why I can't sleep, have trouble focusing, and have trouble relaxing. I knew that I'd dealt with my heart issue for longer than I needed to, but what was done was done, and everything was going to be normal again. But while lying there—maybe eating some pudding, maybe talking to Mom and Dad—I felt a thump in my heart that was harder than it should have been. If I had to write it out, what I felt was something like "thum-thump, thum-thump, THUMP . . . pause . . . thum-thump, thum-thump," and that wasn't normal. I informed the doctor about what I'd felt, after telling my parents. The doctor told me that it was normal, and not to worry. I'd just had a heart procedure. My heart had to heal. It would make sense that I'd feel some wonky things until healing had 100 percent taken place. Objectively, it made sense. But there was something in the back of my mind that I couldn't ignore.

Doctors had told me things were normal before when I didn't think they were, and I had been right—things had not been normal. I was positive that my heart should not have been jackhammering for no reason at all. I was as positive of that as I was that my irregular heartbeat was not from growing pains. It felt dismissive and, frankly, condescending, even though I know it wasn't meant that way. "You're just a kid, you'll grow out of it." Going forward, due to my experience with SVT, my entire mind-set changed significantly. I could not trust doctors. I could only trust myself. I knew my body better than anyone, and so, as had been proven, no one knew the right answer but me. If somebody agreed with me about what was going on, I would listen to them. If somebody did not agree, they were incorrect, and I couldn't trust them. If I'd been right before, I would be right again. I didn't know it at the time, but even though there was something going on with my heart, benign though it was, there was something much worse going on in my mind. I had an illness brought on by that little voice on my shoulder, whispering into my ear, feeding me all the lines, convincing me all the worries were real. Telling me that everything I thought about my body was right, no matter what anybody said.

THREE
WE DO IT OVER AND OVER AGAIN

I'm sitting by the pool in my backyard. Dad used to tell me that the water was calming. He lived that truth. Whenever we were near a body of water, Dad would usually sit by it, remembering his childhood and how it was to live in that sort of peace on the trapline, or maybe simply taking it in, to try to exist within the moment, to strive for that hush in your body. That's why I sit by the water. It's like I'm constantly trying to reclaim the calm I felt when I was on Black Water, an ancestral trapline, with Dad. I didn't even look for my alprazolam that day; usually, if I'm off by five minutes from when I'm supposed to take it, I start to panic. There are loungers at the southeast corner of the pool, and that's where I'm sitting. I'm distracted from typing because I keep looking at a moth that somehow landed on the water's surface and now can't save itself. Like a slow heartbeat, it flutters its wings every few seconds to try to escape and fails. When it flutters its wings, the vibration sends concentric circles, as though a pebble has been thrown into the pool. It's pretty. It sounds ridiculous, but I envy the moth because even though it can't fly away from the water, it's not panicking. It has no concept of death. It's reacting instinctually. *How would that feel*, I think, *to be stuck like*

that and not feel an unreasonable desperation to become unstuck?
To not feel such desperation that it sends unpleasant sensations
through my body that seem beyond my control.

Fight or flight.

Flight.

For probably fifteen years or more now, I've been doing this
thing that I call body scanning. It's not something I perform sub-
consciously or even sporadically. It's constant. I often say (I've
already said it here) that I wouldn't wish anxiety on my worst
enemy. Not the type I have and not any type whatsoever, for
that matter, because each iteration of anxiety or mental health
illness is a cousin to another. Sometimes it feels as if you can't
have one without the other. Many people who live with anxiety
live with a condition called OCD, or obsessive-compulsive disorder. It's a disorder where a person (like me) has uncontrollable, never-ending compulsions that they need to repeat over
and over and over again. I think of *As Good As It Gets*, a movie
starring Jack Nicholson. He taps either side of his slippers with
his toes a certain number of times before sliding his feet into
them. He locks and unlocks his door a precise number of times
when he shuts it or before he opens it. He uses a soap bar only
once when washing his hands and then throws it away. This is
the extreme, but in the game of anxiety, there's not much sepa-
ration between one obsessive act and another; they come from
the same place.

Sometimes I feel crazy, and sometimes I feel as though it's a
wonder I'm not crazy, given how often I scan my body for symptoms. It's not an exaggeration to say that I constantly check my

body for symptoms. Non-stop. I don't know how I get anything done. Even now, sitting by the pool, I'm scanning. I notice a flutter in my chest. I notice pressure in my head. I notice soreness in my neck. There's a slight ache in my left rib cage, just below my heart and to the side. The small victory I seek is to not google any of these symptoms but rather to engage in self-talk and rationalize the symptoms away. It's a constant war consisting of a thousand battles, some that I win and some that I lose.

The flutter in your chest results from a premature ventricular contraction, which is benign; you've had hundreds of thousands of them, and you know that.

You didn't sleep well last night, you're tired, you almost fell asleep while driving an hour ago, and your head feels pressure because you need rest, you always need rest, and you never allow yourself to get it.

Your neck is sore because you golfed with Cole yesterday, and you haven't golfed since Dad died, which means your body hasn't moved like that in almost four years.

Has it been four years since Dad passed away? How did that happen? How did time move so quickly? Your ribs hurt near your heart because your heart is aching. You told Cole yesterday that you want him to remember golfing with you, like you remember golfing with his grandfather.

You're too much of a coward to give him those memories.
You are not present when you golf with your son. You are
too wrapped up in your bodily sensations. You pay more
attention to the way your heart is beating than to your son.

You are pathetic.

You could say that this is spiralling; it's a sterling example of how my brain works. Not only am I constantly trying to rationalize symptoms that I often manifest via anxiety, but at the same time, I'm trying to keep my thoughts under control so that they don't fan out and create ripples, like concentric circles, that eventually will turn into tidal waves. I am stuck in a pool, but I know that I am, and I am struggling to fly but I can't, nor can I accept that truth. The moth has stopped struggling; its wings aren't fluttering any longer. The pool water is still, a perfect reflection of the sky.

I have two clear memories of my grandparents' basement that link to my anxiety and different kinds of fear. One of my favourite picture books is called *My Mama Says There Aren't Any Zombies, Ghosts, Vampires, Creatures, Demons, Monsters, Fiends, Goblins, or Things*, and it is almost as creepy as Maurice Sendak's *Outside Over There*, incidentally my other favourite picture book. In *My Mama Says*, a mother keeps telling a child about everyday things that are often wrong. She has her son carry a heavy grocery bag and argues with the boy when he says the bag is too heavy for him to carry. They go back and forth for an entire page. *I can't. You can. I can't. You can. I can't. You can, she told me.* On the page turn, the boy, named Nick, drops the grocery bag, and the eggs break when they hit the ground. The refrain is *Sometimes even mamas make mistakes*, and that logic is used to explain why, when the boy's mother tells him there's no such thing as zombies, he isn't certain he can believe her. After all, she was wrong about the groceries and several other things. And if she was wrong about this, then she could most definitely be wrong about the existence of a Thing in the yard whispering to the boy that it was coming to get him.

Life imitates art in more ways than one.

That book is one of my favourites, and also one of the scariest I've ever read. The most frightening figure in a parade of apparitions and creatures is the Fiend, who, *maybe*, is in the lower bunk of Nick's bed, sniffing around for a boy to eat. The words are scary, but the illustration of the Fiend is even more frightening, with his long snout, sharp teeth, top hat with a scary face on *it* for good measure, furry eyebrows, polka dot pants (somehow terrifying within the context of the story), and high heels (ditto). Fiends haunted my childhood. In my belief system, they mostly existed in my grandparents' basement when I was alone down there. But I also used to check under my bed before I went to sleep, anywhere I lay my head. I used to sprint up a flight of stairs in any home in case a Fiend was tiptoeing up the steps behind me. To be honest, I'm still scared of Fiends. I still take the stairs quickly, when moving from the basement to the first floor, and when it's dark and late at night.

The power of stories.

The other memory I have, and hold closest of all, is of a thunderstorm, a power outage, cribbage, and a piano song. As a child, I spent a week or two every summer in Melita, staying with my grandparents alone. And while there were things I struggled with, like Fiends, or a bully who used to chase me around the pool and shout out racist names because I was brown-skinned, I looked forward to my time in Melita; I've always felt most at ease in a small town (aside from there being Fiends in basements, and, according to my cousin, kidnappers across the street who watched kids from their attic window). One night, I was playing cribbage with my grandfather, a game, like golf, I could never beat him at. By that time, he was suffering from ALS and had lost control of his tongue. He spoke through a computer that made him sound like Stephen Hawking and was fed through a tube because he couldn't swallow. And so, it was a quiet game. I didn't talk much to him; I learned the art of having a conversation that allowed him to respond by writing notes on a yellow-papered notepad that he kept on his person rather than typing words into the machine that made him sound like a robot. One day, in Winnipeg, I asked Grandpa if he was scared (this was near the end), and I'll never forget his response, in perfect cursive.

Yes.

"Does it hurt, Grandpa?"

Yes, it hurts.

A storm was brewing outside. It wasn't quite dark out yet, but the threatening storm clouds made it feel that way. They blotted out the sun. We were playing under the basement lighting, on a card table. On the wall to the right, there was shelving that boasted Grandpa's collection of carvings; he liked to make boots and ducks. A few steps away to the left, at the bottom of the stairs and flush against the wall, was an old, upright piano that my great-grandfather, a composer, used to own. I may have inherited some of that skill, though in typical lazy teenage fashion, I'd not done much with the ability I'd been gifted. I got up to the eighth grade in piano but quit early into high school, and never took lessons again. At that stage of my childhood, however, though I didn't much care for playing other works, I did enjoy composing some of my own songs, more contemporary music. Some of my songs had lyrics, some of them did not. Behind Grandpa, there was his desk at the northwest corner, and his gun rack on the south wall, which displayed his hunting rifles. Behind me, there was a small tube television where I tried to watch movies through static, a coffee table stacked with books, including the Bible with a bookmark that was really a Polaroid shot of a tauntaun action figure, and two recliners. We were several minutes into a game when through the bright fluorescent lighting and a tiny basement window we saw a flash of lightning followed by an eardrum-shattering crack of thunder. The lights went out, and Grandpa and I were sitting in the dark, in the silence, only the patter of rain outside and the occasional rumble from thunder breaking the hush. I put down my cards; Grandpa put down his cards. My hands were crossed together on the table, on my side of the cribbage board. I heard it slide over, out of the way, and then Grandpa's bony hands rested on mine. He was comforting me. He knew I was afraid of the dark, and that the fear was compounded by being in the basement. I'd repeatedly asked him and Grandma for reassurance that there was no such thing as Fiends. But I wasn't afraid, not with Grandpa there with me. Then I thought of Grandpa's note, in response to my question.

"Are you afraid?"

Yes.

I may have been projecting my own fear of the darkness onto my grandfather. I may have imagined his hands shaking, ever slightly.

Are you afraid?

Yes.

I was never the most gifted student academically; I just wasn't that interested in school. The same was true of piano, although my grades were better with it. I got First Class Honours on a few of my piano exams and Honours on a couple of others. I liked the piano. I liked it even more when I wrote my own stuff. At the time of the storm in Melita, sitting in the darkness of my grandparents' basement, I'd been working on a sad, particularly haunting song. It wasn't finished, but I'd been practising it so often that what I had written was memorized. And I didn't need light. I slipped my hands out from underneath my grandfather's hands, patted them once to let him know I wasn't going anywhere far, and then sat at the piano, opened the fallboard, and placed my fingers on the keys.

The sound of the rain washed away for a brief while, and the rolling thunder fell to a whisper. I heard Grandpa shift in his seat to turn towards me, even though he couldn't see me. I played my song, pressing the keys with precision, making the notes soften with the una corda pedal, and then stretching them out with the damper pedal. For a few minutes, all there was was the song, and I don't know if it pushed out the darkness or welcomed it in as a part of the music. Either way, there was a calmness that surrounded us. I could feel it, and I think Grandpa could feel it. When I finished playing the song, as though it had been timed this way, the lights came back on. I turned around to see Grandpa watching me. We exchanged a look, tiny sounds reintroduced themselves, and I took my place at the card table, where we continued our game as if nothing had happened.

Grandpa died within the year from ALS, two days after my birthday, on January 14, 1998.

While this sounds like a positive memory, one about connection and facing fears together, it showed me that a grown-up could be afraid and that death did come for you.

Around the time of my grandfather's sickness and his death, I exhibited behaviours of health anxiety without recognizing them as such. I knew what was happening, don't get me wrong. I knew that when I had a twitching eyelid, I'd start worrying about getting the same disease that my grandfather had died from. I didn't know how problematic the machinations of my worry would become. The only thing I did know was that ALS could be hereditary, and somewhere, I'm not sure where (I refuse to google it), I read that it skipped a generation. That meant, in my mind, in big flickering neon lights, there was a sign that read: "SOMEBODY IN YOUR GENERATION WILL GET ALS." There weren't many options, so it was more than likely going to be me.

The prospect was terrifying. I'd seen what the disease had done to my grandfather and the impact his sickness had had on my family. I found myself replaying all of that in my mind, only it was me in place of my grandfather, and my family had to deal with my physical decline. And I knew there was no way I would handle the disease with as much grace as my grandfather had. He was scared, yes. It hurt him, yes. But not once did he place that burden on anybody else; if other people in my family felt pain from his disease, it was a pain we put on ourselves as a result of our love for him and empathy for the inevitability of his death. I daydreamed, in a totally messed-up way, because it was wishing prolonged suffering on somebody, that he could survive for decades with it, just like Stephen Hawking. But the truth was, Hawking was an outlier. Today, the average survival time for somebody with ALS is two to five years; I don't know what it would've been thirty years ago.

If all of this comes across as a rambling, messy thought process, it ought to. That's what my brain looks like in its worst state of anxiety. It's a traffic jam, a thousand cars backed up on the freeway, drivers honking and swearing at each other and a thirty-minute delay to get one block farther. It's a whole lot of spinning wheels without much positive movement forward. Mostly, it's reversing backwards into oncoming traffic. Other people move forward; you move backwards. You are left behind and alone.

During my grandfather's illness and after his death, I would obsessively scan my body for any sort of involuntary twitch, most often an eyelid, or uncontrollable muscle spasms: my bicep, my thigh, or near the heel of my foot. And good lord, I freaked out if my tongue did anything out of the ordinary, since that was where my grandfather's sickness started. But despite my certainty that I would 100 percent contract the disease, years went by and I did not (knock on wood) get ALS. Rather, I was left to deal with my heart condition. That should've ended as soon as it was fixed with the EPS and catheter ablation. The procedure was almost 100 percent effective; there was no reason why I would be one of the few people it didn't work on, and even if it didn't work, I could get it done again. I'm not sure of the math, but if you got a procedure that was usually 97 percent effective done twice, it meant that unless you were the unluckiest person in the world, your heart problem would be corrected.

There was that thump, though.

That thump and then a pause in recovery after the procedure.

The doctor told me it was normal, which seemed logical because I'd been through heart surgery, non-invasive though it was. But there was a recurring thought I couldn't shake, a thought I'd carry with me, that I still carry with me even today. It's a thought I fight more than anything else in my life.

My doctor was wrong about my heart, and I was right. That means I can be right about other issues in my body even when a doctor, or multiple doctors, tells me otherwise.

If there is a petri dish of mental health disorders, of health anxiety, that's it right there. That's what makes all those little monsters in the mental health disorder family grow and infect.

The worry about twitching muscles was always there, has remained there, and will likely always be present in my life. As clear and present as my grandfather's note that told me he was scared. Just recently, my bottom eyelid was twitching for a week straight, and it would not stop. I took a video of the twitching and sent it to my doctor, and she told me that it was normal, and that it was a product of exhaustion and stress. Objectively, I knew she was right. I *was* stressed—I was working on two books at the same time (one of them was this one), editing another, travelling to two different cities, and working as an editorial director for a new Indigenous-run imprint, all while juggling life as a father of five (thank god for Jill)—and I was exhausted. But as long as my eyelid was twitching, it didn't matter what my doctor said. I had ALS, and soon it would spread, most probably to my tongue. My eyelid stopped twitching recently, and I do not, as far as I know, have a degenerative, incurable disease. (Other people do, and sometimes I feel like it's an insult to them to internalize their struggles and allow those fears to dictate my actions.)

Immediately after the procedure in London, Ontario, though, it was not twitching muscles or that odd heartbeat with the thump and the pause that caused me the most concern. Rather, it was pressure headaches, which should have been innocuous. Everybody gets all kinds of headaches for a million different reasons, and most of those reasons aren't anything to worry about.

My headaches started off similarly in that I had them, and they bothered me, but I didn't think I was going to die from them. Headaches come and go, but after several days, I found mine was not going anywhere. It was a weird headache, too. There was no pain. I never had to take Tylenol or Advil. It was just pressure, a weight pressing down on top of my forehead. Like I had with my heart condition, I tried to find natural remedies for it. Most commonly, I'd stretch my neck religiously. Obsessively. I'd stretch it for exactly thirty seconds to either side and then from back to front for half a minute in each direction. I figured (and by then, the internet was definitely a thing) it was happening due to tight muscles. If I consistently stretched my neck, it would follow that my headache would resolve. It didn't.

When my headache was still there after weeks, I started to worry, especially when I was told, again, that it was not a tumour. I was sure that it was, and my mind kept replaying my heart condition scenario. I'd thought I had a heart condition, but my doctor did not, and it turned out that I had one. And so, if I thought I had a tumour and my doctor did not, I was probably right about that as well. The problem was that I had no control over what tests, if any, I was given to confirm whether I had a tumour. At one point, I got a CT scan of my sinuses to see if they were causing my headache. I had a deviated septum (which, according to the ear, nose, and throat specialist, a lot of people have), but that didn't explain the pressure headache. The CT scan was a test I didn't want; it wasn't imaging my brain, which is what I believed I needed. And so, without any confirmation of the fact that I didn't have a tumour, I kept right on believing that I did—and I continued to worry that it would grow and grow, and that the pressure would get worse and worse until, eventually, it would be terminal, and I would be dead. On the off chance that I did not have a tumour, I kept seeking treatment for my headache, hoping against hope that it would go away.

I should mention, at this point, that my headache was likely not as bad as I thought. This is not to say that it didn't bother me, that it wasn't disruptive to my daily life, because it was. It was not fun. And by extension, this is not to say that anybody who feels symptoms that are not normal is imagining or intentionally exaggerating them. Trust me. I've been there. Nothing is more real than what is going on in your body, and anxiety, depression, and our mental health issues can create real symptoms. If you have a headache, you have a headache. If you have premature ventricular contractions, then you have premature ventricular contractions. They'll show up on an ECG. It's not like an apparition that you think is there but won't co-operate with your request for them to knock three times if they're present. What I *am* saying is that when you focus on something so intently, whatever you're focusing on cannot help but feel more pronounced. If you're focusing on your heartbeat, you'll notice it more, and if there's an irregularity to its rhythm, that irregularity, because of the anxiety it causes from the attention, might be exacerbated. If you have a pressure headache and all you're doing is focusing on your head and nothing else, not only is that all you're going to notice, but it will also seem worse and might get worse. In my experience, all of the symptoms I've zeroed in on have, without fail, gotten worse. It's a vicious cycle. The more you pay attention to your symptoms, the worse they get, the more you worry about them, the worse they get, and on and on and on it goes. And no testing will ever be enough to convince you that those symptoms are not what you *think* they are. To break out of this vicious cycle, you need to get to a place where you notice something in your body, you rationalize it objectively, and, if you need to, you get tested for it—and once those test results come back, you trust them. Often, they are accurate. *Far* more often than they are not, in fact. And I will repeat this a million times: Do not, under any circumstance, google your symptoms. Googling is not an accurate assessment tool.

My headache didn't go away, no matter what I did. Stretching didn't work. Massage therapy didn't work either. I couldn't get out of my head long enough for a massage to relax me, so that treatment failed on two fronts. At the time, I worked in the Bodily Injury Department for Manitoba Public Insurance (MPI), assessing claimants' permanent impairment(s) from motor vehicle accidents, which could range from scarring to loss of movement to head injuries, and what sort of treatment would be needed for soft tissue injuries—things like acupuncture, physiotherapy, chiropractic, athletic therapy, and so on. We worked with medical professionals from all these disciplines who helped determine need, including chiropractors. I tried chiropractic treatment for my pressure headache. During my treatment, which involved something called Active Release Therapy, I also received a high-velocity neck adjustment. The chiropractor cracked it once, said,

"Wait, no, that's not quite it," did it again, said, "Yep, there it is," then moved on.

On the way home, driving down Portage Avenue within minutes of leaving the chiropractor's office, I started to feel flush. It was the weirdest sensation. I'd never had a high-velocity neck adjustment before, so I had no reference point, and no idea if it was normal. It felt like a wave of warmth was spreading through my entire body, from my toes all the way to the top of my head, and I started to black out. I pulled over into a parking lot until I was sure I would stay conscious, and then drove to my house. I went to my bedroom and lay on the bed. I'd gone to the chiropractor without much hope, but now I'd added a new worry: my headache was worse, and I was sure the high-velocity neck adjustment was going to cause a stroke. This might've been my first foray into internet symptom checking. When I typed "high-velocity neck adjustment," a hurricane of scary risks was thrown at me. *The high-velocity thrust used in cervical manipulation can significantly strain carotid and vertebral vessels. Once a dissection has occurred, the risk of thrombus formation, ischemic stroke, paralysis, and even death is drastically increased.* I ignored any information that discounted the worrisome search results. *Chiropractic adjustment is safe when it's performed by someone trained and licensed to deliver chiropractic care. Serious complications associated with chiropractic adjustment are overall rare.* I even shrugged off reassurance from the chiropractor himself, who later told me, when I recounted my experience, that what I had felt was my body releasing built-up toxins.

I began to spiral. I had a thrombus formation and was in the middle of going through all the stages—constriction of a blood vessel, formation of a platelet plug, activation of the coagulation cascade, and then the formation of the final clot, which sounds awful. I was going to become paralyzed, from the neck down, and live the rest of my life in a wheelchair. Seeing *ischemic stroke* confirmed my initial worry of having a stroke, which was likely already in progress. And there was the D word. Death. I spent that night not thinking that I might die but being *sure* that I would. I tucked my kids into bed like it was the last time I would see them. I watched Jill while she slept, savouring everything about her, counting eyelashes and thinking, *I love you*, for each one. There was one positive that I likely wouldn't have dared to articulate at the time, but I can see clearly now. If that was going to be my last night on earth, it meant that at least there wouldn't be pressure in my head any longer. It was a small consolation.

Surprisingly, I woke up the next morning, but the pressure in my head would dog me for years. There seemed to be nothing I could do but live with it, and making matters worse, few things could distract me from it. I worked respite (when someone looks after the person you typically care for, so that you can have a break) a few times for a family in Transcona who had a young man with no short-term memory. He'd be up most of the night, and I had to remind him to go to sleep (because he'd forget that he had to) and make sure that he didn't wander out of the house. The job required me to stay up for hours, until I was relieved by his parents. I snacked and watched movies, checked on the guy at least once an hour, and did my best to push through my head-ache, which, at the time, was the worst it had ever been. I drove home, from Transcona to the West End, about a thirty-minute trip, crying most of the way, wondering when I'd ever feel clear in the head, wondering how long I could keep hoping that mirac-ulously the pressure in my head would be gone. But bigger than the wondering and the hoping was the fear. My doctor and other doctors I saw failed to recognize what was really happening in my head. I was dying, and there was no way I could prove it.

Then, one day, I finally got the chance to see what was hap-pening. Back when I wasn't afraid of exercising, I biked to work, which was a ten-kilometre ride. I took the same route each day, with no deviation (which was, as you may guess, another early sign of my mental health struggles, in particular my OCD). My path led me down Cambridge Street, where I eventually had to cross Fleet Avenue. At the intersection, there is a four-way stop. I like to follow rules, for the most part, and especially on a bike, where you're vulnerable, with only a helmet to protect you (back then, there were no bike lanes). When traffic was around, I never coasted through a stop sign on my bike. I came to a full stop, made sure it was safe, and then kept going. When I approached the stop sign heading southbound on Cambridge Avenue, I saw a van approaching a fair way off to my right. As was customary for me, I stopped and pedalled forward, feeling it was safe to do so. It was too late when I noticed the van on my right was not going to stop. I was already in its path and couldn't speed up and get out of the way because I wasn't fast enough. I yelled some-thing futile at the van, like, "Hey!" and braced for impact. The van slammed on its brakes, but when it hit me with its front driver-side bumper, it must have been going at least thirty kilometres per hour. The next several minutes remain a blur, but there are images that present themselves in strobe light flashes. The van hits my bike but somehow, initially, misses my body. The force of the collision is enough to throw me off my bike against the van. I stick out my right arm as if I'm a running back trying to straight-arm a defender, and my hand and wrist crack the van's front windshield. I topple over the van's roof and fall onto the concrete behind it. I watch, in shock, and so without immediate pain, as the van comes to a stop twenty feet past the intersection.

The pain came as people started to crowd around me, including the driver, who'd gotten out of her vehicle to check on my condition. She would later claim, according to my adjuster at Manitoba Public Insurance, that I blew the stop sign, that she'd come to a complete stop and had only started to pull forward (thanks to something called "reverse onus," where, in a collision with a pedestrian or bicycle, the motorist has to prove it was not their fault, which she could not do, the driver was assessed 100 percent responsible for the accident). Somebody called 9-1-1 while I was on the ground. The pain escalated with every passing second and was concentrated in my right wrist, arm, and shoulder, as well as my head. I felt something up there besides pressure for the first time in a long time. Apparently, after rolling over top of the van, I fell directly on my head. As it turns out, bike helmets work. With my head hurting like it did, I couldn't imagine what would have happened if I'd been biking without any protection.

I was taken to Victoria General Hospital, where Jill met me soon after, and a battery of tests was administered to assess the extent of my injuries. Considering I'd been struck by a van travelling that fast, I'd been lucky. I swore my wrist was broken, but it wasn't. The doctor thought it had likely been sprained, and to be honest, I wasn't too concerned about it with or without a break. Aside from the road rash, my wrist hurt the least (this is ironic since it was the injury that lasted the longest; I still have trouble with it). My shoulder was torn, and I wore a sling while it healed. And there was my head. As the hours wore on, as the tests came and went, and as the pain began to improve, I thought more and more about my head. I hoped the doctor would send me for a CT scan to see if my brain had been injured. After all, I'd landed on it following a collision with a van. A concussion wasn't what was on my mind, though. I probably had suffered a minor concussion. How could I not have? But if the doctor sent me for a scan of my brain, she would see, inadvertently, the tumour that had been growing in my head for the last few years. The bike accident began to feel like a good thing. I'd read numerous stories about people who'd gone to the hospital for one thing and, through testing, had discovered something life-threatening that wouldn't have been discovered otherwise.

After going through all the testing for my other injuries, the doctor entered my hospital room and asked about my head. I tried to give her answers that weren't quite a lie but weren't exactly true. When she asked if I knew what day it was, I wasn't about to tell her I didn't, because I did. But a slight hesitation before answering? That might give her cause for concern. I provided a calculated answer to every question, designed solely to get myself in for a CT scan so I'd finally get images of my brain and that pesky tumour. But try as I did, I was not given a CT scan, and I left the hospital with no more answers than I'd had before the accident. My engagement with the emergency room doctor had become about my pressure headache, not about the fact that I'd received actual injuries from getting T-boned by a van.

But that's the sickness of it.

Worry or any other mental health affliction becomes all-consuming. No matter how small it starts off, it ends up being enormous. It grows exponentially and takes over every action, every thought, and every moment. By doing so, it prevents you from living in the moment, from experiencing life for what it can be; instead, it has you living an entirely different life. I deserve better. So do you.

There's a saying. Ninety-nine percent of things you worry about never happen. Honestly, the number is likely higher than that. During any given day, I worry about hundreds of things, and on most days, none of the things I worry about happen. Math isn't my strong suit, but I'm pretty sure it's more like 99.9 percent of the things you worry about never happen. I feel as though anxiety and worry are like throwing darts blindfolded. If you throw a few hundred darts, you will eventually hit a bull's eye. But I'll tell you something: worry never stops anything from happening. What's going to happen will happen, whether you worry about it or not.

The irony is that worry can, conversely, cause things to happen. It can wreak havoc on your body as much as it can mess with your mind. Wreck your nerves. And once your nerves are damaged, it's difficult, if not impossible, for them to work properly again. Is it any coincidence that my brothers, both older than me, continue to have black hair while my hair turns white? It would be easy for me to say that all that white hair is because I've worked two or three jobs for a long time and have five children, but that would be a lie. Sure, the stress of work and kids is probably a part of it, but my mental health has played a more significant role.

There's just been so much goddamn worry in my life, and the hook of it is that it was, and is, completely avoidable. I didn't have to spend one second worrying. I really didn't. It's not reasonable to expect that you can avoid worry altogether, but to worry to the extent that it literally changes your appearance and your health? That's not good. You can actually worry your life away. You know, if I look at my life objectively, particularly over the last fourteen years, I can say that I've done well (while recognizing that I'll never rest on my laurels). But in the same breath, I can also say that I could have enjoyed everything so much more if I'd just stopped allowing anxiety (which, in turn, has led to more severe ailments) to get in the way.

Take my years-long battle with anxiety over my pressure headache. My obsessive worry dictated what I did, how I thought, the relationships I had, everything, for an unreasonable period of time. And that brain tumour I was sure I had? The one I was sure was killing me? The one that led me to literally write letters to my children in the event of my death (something I've done more than once)? The one that kept me up at night playing the "What would people say at my funeral" game or the "Who would come to my funeral" game? It never materialized. I would love to tell you that I came to my senses. That one day, I woke up and thought, *What am I doing? This is ridiculous. No matter how my head feels, I will get up and live my life.* That would have been the right approach. And in living my life, in getting up and doing things I did not feel like doing, though I also wanted to do them, I guarantee you that I would have noticed my brain tumour less (and for *brain tumour*, you can substitute any worry you're obsessed over, whether health-related or otherwise). I would love to tell you that, but I just wasn't there yet. This was at the beginning of my serious mental health illness, not at the end. What happened was that one day, about seven years later, I woke up and I accepted that if I had had a brain tumour, I probably would have been dead by then. I figured that my pressure headache had been caused by something else, something chronic, certainly, but not terminal. Ironically, one of the leading causes of my pressure headache was worry over what might have been going on in my brain. If it's frustrating to read how scattershot and nonsensical this is, it's even more frustrating having lived through it. It's not that I don't have a rational brain that tells me the likely reality of the situation; it's that I have another part of my brain that screams an alternate reality, and because it's screaming, I focus on and listen to it rather than the healthier voice.

*

I have a confession to make. I could tell the same story over and over again, and there would be minimal deviation, other than the fact that you can take out *brain tumour* and replace it with *Lou Gehrig's disease* or *stroke* or *HIV/AIDS* (I made my doctor test me for it in the nineties) or *Parkinson's disease* (when I heard that Michael J. Fox had it) or almost every form of cancer, including stomach cancer (which my uncle Daniel died from—on my wife's side). Yeah, here's how much anxiety controls you and how much you become willing to do whatever it tells you to do. I went through a period where I was bloated constantly, constipated, and never felt like eating. As a result, I lost almost twenty pounds in short order. There are pictures of me during those weeks in which I look so thin, it's scary. I was so sure that my stomach problems were caused by cancer that I convinced my doctor to send me for an upper gastrointestinal endoscopy. I went to St. Boniface Hospital for it, and because I was (stop me if you've heard this one) afraid of being put under, I opted to have the test done without any medication. It was the worst experience of my life; it felt like I was choking to death on something for ten minutes straight. I probably don't have to tell you the test results (the specialist told me, essentially, that I needed to take antacids, if anything), but what I can tell you is that, like my pressure headache, the stomach problems I was having were almost certainly caused by my mental health illness, as opposed to any cancer.

After the test was over, and the doctor who'd stuck the black metal tube down my throat told me that he didn't think he'd seen anything but was going to send off the biopsy to confirm, Jill came to pick me up. She was doing everything she could to get me to eat. On the way home from the hospital, she took me to Boon Burger, a vegan burger place on Sherbrook Street. I ordered a plain, vegan, gluten-free burger and, with encouragement, ate the whole thing. Over time, I ate more and more, eventually gaining back the weight I'd lost. Atypically, after being reassured by the doctor and, later, the test results, I conceded that I likely did not have stomach cancer. That doesn't mean that my stomach issues have resolved. In my experience, stomach issues are the most common symptom of anxiety. Not cancer. Anxiety. I've had more periods of bloating than I can count. I take Gas-X regularly, even now, when I feel any bloating episode coming on. I always have a little tube of Tums in my backpack that I dip into when I think I'm getting heartburn. And I get these pains in my lower intestine that feel as though I'm in labour, followed by diarrhea that can keep me up for hours. And none of this is caused by the flu. It's caused by worry. Worry that affects my mind, that affects my nerves, that affects my body, that causes symptoms, that causes worry that affects my mind, that affects my nerves, that affects my body, that causes symptoms . . . The cycle continues until you break it. But that worry, that anxiety, that depression, that cycle is a diamond. The hardest material on earth. How do you break something like that? How do you break it when you don't know it's happening to you?

One of my favourite movies of all time is *The Shawshank Redemption*. It's a great film; almost every scene is perfect, but I love it for one line. I'm like that, I guess. I latch on to something that elicits a visceral reaction, a big emotion, tears, or joy. After my dad died, every father-son movie made me drown in a pool of saltwater tears. *Guardians of the Galaxy Vol. 2*; *Onward*. I watch the darts scene from *Ted Lasso* almost every day. I watch the speech from *The Great Dictator* to find inspiration for my work: "Let us fight for a new world—a decent world that will give men a chance to work—that will give youth a future and old age a security. By the promise of these things, brutes have risen to power. But they lie! They do not fulfil that promise. They never will!" Add music to it, and I'm ready to take on the world. In *Shawshank*, there's a scene where Red says, "Get busy living, or get busy dying," and I find those words applicable to my mental health journey. I try to live by those words now. Sometimes I fail, sometimes I succeed, yet they are always something to strive for. Because of what I've been through, I'm more and more capable of success; though I still fail, the goal is always to succeed more and fail less while not getting down on myself for those failures.

As the first decade of the 2000s ended, I wasn't ready to ingrain those words into my journey. I'm not even sure that I would have acknowledged I was on a journey. I had been through hard times, whether brought on by myself or an extra node in my heart, but not a headache or a twitching eyelid or a rapidly beating heart or some bloating forced me to get busy living or dying. These things were inconveniences and scary, but I was always, at least, *functional*.

There's something called the pressure cooker analogy. I'm quite good at bottling up my emotions and feelings. For the most part, I think Robertsons excel at this sort of thing. My wife hates arguing with me because I often refuse to fight. Rather than fight, I push it all down. You can bottle a lot of things up in your body, including worry, and it might work for a while, it might work for years, but eventually, there's too much built up, and you feel like you're going to blow. And more often than not, you do just that.

When I was a kid, I was going through so much crap with my identity and self-confidence that during an argument with my parents and brothers, I punched a hole through the pantry door in our kitchen. I was not a violent kid. I am not a violent man. I have never punched anybody in my entire life. But I put my hand clean through that wooden door. Everything I'd been pushing down exploded. *The longer we deny how we really feel, the bigger that pressure cooker becomes.* And then it erupts, and everything you've been pushing down reveals itself, and you're forced to deal with it and make a profound decision about whether you will struggle with it or live with it. That violent upsurge occurred for me in 2010, and it changed everything. It was my choice whether that change would be for the better or worse.

FOUR
BREAKDOWN

Two thousand and ten should have been a good year. Jill and I had so many life-changing events on the horizon that we were genuinely excited for. At the beginning of 2010, in the middle of winter, there were four certainties. The best of them was that we were expecting our fourth child in late May or early June; we were both relatively sure that it would be close to mid-June because our first three children—Emily, Cole, and Anna—had all been two weeks late.

If we're going in order from most to least important, next up would be that my first published book was coming out in March, and we would have a real live book launch in the fall. Up until that point, I'd only self-published my writing. In 2001, I put out a book (that I will not tell you the title of), and I wrote another one a couple of years later (that I will also not tell you the title of). This book isn't about my publishing journey, even though my entire career as an author has been marked by the most difficult stage of my struggle with mental health issues, so I'll endeavour to keep this short. In 2006, I decided that I wanted to write graphic novels because comics had been so damaging when I was growing up, as much as I loved them. The representation of

Indigenous people was awful, and I thought I could do better, so I decided to fight fire with fire. In partnership with the Helen Betty Osborne Memorial Foundation, I researched, wrote, edited, and designed a graphic novel entitled *The Life of Helen Betty Osborne*. Despite being mostly created by an amateur, the book did good things and sold out all five thousand copies we printed. One day, Catherine Gerbasi, publisher of Portage & Main Press, came across *The Life of Helen Betty Osborne* in a local indie bookstore, picked it up, read it, and decided that she wanted to distribute it, noticing that it had been published independently. When I brought my box of books to the publisher's office, I saw Catherine and her team in the lobby. I asked them if they'd be interested in publishing more graphic novels, and the rest, as they say, is history. The one piece of writing advice I'll give you in this memoir about mental health is that you have to shoot your shot. At any rate, within two years, my first professionally published book, *Stone* (part of the 7 Generations series), was on its way, and we were planning a big event at McNally Robinson Booksellers.

Third, because of the imminent arrival of Lauren Danielle Robertson, Jill and I knew we were outgrowing our house on Lipton Street. It could handle five people, but six? Can we go back to the pressure cooker analogy? We weren't well off at that point in our lives; we often struggled with money and couldn't afford to live anywhere else but in the area we were already in. As luck would have it, we found a place on Banning, exactly one street to the east of Lipton. It was a great move for us, not only because the house was almost twice as big, but because we already knew one of our next-door neighbours; the Nikkels went to the same church as us.

Finally, I was transitioning from my first job with Indigenous communities in Manitoba as a project coordinator in information and communications technology to a federal initiative called Connecting Aboriginals to Manufacturing with Workplace Education Manitoba. Like my dad had done before me, I was going to envision, build, and deliver an entire program that would benefit Indigenous people by opening doorways to finding and sustaining a career in an industry where we were underrepresented.

One of those events happening in a calendar year would be a lot. But four big events, three of which land on many "Most Stressful Life Events" lists (starting a new job, having children, and moving)? That's something else entirely. Still, I was mostly oblivious to the strain building up in my mind and body. Back then, I liked to think I was like my father: cool, calm, and collected. It's funny to look back on that now. I cannot fathom going through life without worrying every second of every day, just as much as I cannot fathom playing basketball for an hour and working up a sweat. Today, I am so in tune with my body that it feels unrealistic, never mind frightening. Nothing happens in my body that I am not acutely aware of. I notice every single anomaly, big or small, and it's exhausting. It's been that way for so long now that I can't imagine not thinking the way I do; I can't grasp how other people don't go through life with a ceaseless inner monologue that never stops, how people go through their days without scanning their body every possible moment. I can't remember being like that.

There were more stressors, too, that were out of my control.

Before the move in April 2010, my maternal grandmother suddenly fell ill. She'd been living in the only house I'd ever known her to live in, at the top of the hill on Ash Street by Veterans Way. My auntie Joan had been living with her for a while after Joan had sold and moved out of her house at the intersection of Campbell and North, across the street from the school my cousin Shayne and I, along with my brother Mike, scaled all the way to the roof on more than one occasion.

Grandma had been dealing with a heart issue. She had been on medication for it. Early in 2010, her heart took a turn for the worse, and it was bad enough that she had to be admitted to Melita Health Centre. She left home to get checked in for treatment, and she never went home again. We drove up to see her in the health centre, Mom and Cam and Mike and me.

When we arrived, we were ushered inside to a waiting room. I remember the quiet while we waited for Grandma. She was being brought to us by one of the nurses. I thought, *How bad is it that she has to be brought to us, that she can't make it on her own?* The last time I'd seen her, which wasn't all that long before this emergency trip to Melita, she looked fine. She was her cute, jovial, lively self. When she laughed, her entire body laughed. We were all in chairs, waiting nervously. I think I sat at the piano that was in the waiting room along with the chairs. Maybe I was thinking of the storm, of sitting in the basement with Grandpa after he'd developed ALS. Maybe I wanted to find that sort of calm again in the face of solemnity. Eventually, after a wait that seemed as long as the trip to Melita, a nurse brought Grandma into the waiting room. Wheeled her into the waiting room, rather. She couldn't walk under her own power. I'd be lying if I told you that I knew what we talked about. All I know is that we didn't say much. Grandma was too weak. Her voice was soft and cracking, like it was a piece of brittle glass, like it might shatter if she spoke too loudly. Grandma was short, but she'd always seemed larger than life to me. She looked small in that waiting room, hunched into the wheelchair, her hands folded on her lap.

People can leave so quickly. Why does it happen like that? Is it selfish that I wished for it to be slower so we could say goodbye for longer?

Grandma couldn't stay with us long. Being out of bed and having whatever brief conversation we'd had took a lot out of her. We all said goodbye when we left. For me, at least, there was a sense that I might not see her again. That this wasn't just *a* goodbye but the *last* goodbye. When Grandpa died, I hadn't seen him for a few months, and I've never been able to forgive myself for not driving out to visit him during his final days, when he'd lost the ability to walk. At least I got to say goodbye this time. I told her I loved her, and just like I used to do with Grandpa, I kissed the top of her head. Her hair was dry and thin; I could feel her scalp against my lips. The nurse took her away, and we left the waiting room one by one, then returned home to Winnipeg. The journey to Melita had gotten shorter as I got older, but that drive, on that day, seemed to take forever.

I'd never spent much time at Melita Health Centre before, and my time there with Grandma had been the longest. When I was a kid, it scared me. I used to bike past it daily on my way to the pool or the golf course. Most of the time, there was nobody outside, and so passing by was like passing by any other building. I didn't think much of it. One afternoon, though, a man was outside in a blue hospital gown, a housecoat over top, and a pair of slippers. He had a tray in front of him with food and a nurse at his side. Nothing seemed odd about it until I took a closer look and saw the man's vacant eyes. The place I used to imagine beyond the stars when I was a kid, wandering through the house in the dark, aimless—that's where that man was. His body was in front of the hospital; his mind was not. The nurse fed him something soft and red. It might've been Jell-O; it might've been strawberry jam. Something red was dripping from his mouth, along with a trail of saliva. The poor guy was sick, I knew that, but the sight of him unsettled me. When I saw someone like that, I couldn't help but picture myself in their position. I couldn't help but think that being that person, one day, was an inevitability. That one day, I'd get ill. I'd end up in a hospital. It had happened to Grandpa. Now, more than a decade after his death, it had happened to Grandma.

She hung on for months. She was tough. Maybe that was the Irish in her. She was tough like Grandpa. On the night my grandfather died, he went with dignity and elegance, even though he was scared and in pain. And it's hard for me to wrap my head around that. I've imagined myself having ALS like Grandpa more times than I care to count. I wonder how I would deal with it, knowing that, bit by bit, parts of me would be stolen. The movement of a finger. Of a tongue. The ability to speak. To eat. The ability to walk. Eventually, I would completely depend on others for the most mundane, rudimentary activities. Buttoning up a shirt. Tying my shoes. Lifting my head, for the love of god. I play scenes in my head where I keep writing, but I'm doing it by the movement of my eyes. I'm not sure I'd be able to write that way. I'm not sure I'd be able to live through the disease with the poise and courage Grandpa did. I'm not sure I'd be able to rise above the fear, especially considering how much the smallest fears have controlled my life. I would crumple. I would fold into nothing, like a Murphy bed. People always say things like, "You don't know how much strength you have. You'd be surprised how brave you are."

I don't know about that.

Grandma was moved to Brandon General Hospital—the place of my birth, all the way back in January 1977—when the facilities in Melita couldn't give her the treatment and attention she needed. What an odd thing for a building to be filled with so much life and so much death. My uncle Rob flew in to spend time with his mother and his sister (my mom). They spent a lot of time in Brandon while Jill and I crept closer to Lauren's due date. Grandma was leaving this world; somebody else was coming into it. I wanted her to hang on long enough to meet my daughter. I really did.

Jill and I had taken to having our children at home rather than at the hospital. Emily and Cole were born at the Women's Hospital beside the Health Sciences Centre, which was fine. We were cared for, and for a hypochondriac, having nurses and doctors close at hand was reassuring. The thing is, when you have health anxiety, the worry you have for your health often extends to worry for the health of others. You don't just google symptoms for yourself; you google symptoms for your neighbour's cat. Yet Anna was born at our house on Lipton Street, in our bedroom, with at least three midwives helping out, which was beautiful, and we wanted to do the same for Lauren.

Nobody told Lauren she was supposed to arrive two weeks after her due date. She had her own schedule in mind, albeit just a week earlier than anticipated. In the middle of the night on June 3, 2010, Jill walked into Anna's room, where I was sleeping for some reason. Jill joked that I was trying to get my beauty sleep; I said that you had to be beautiful to sleep like that. I saw her silhouette in the doorway, her face lit softly by moonlight filtering through the bedroom window. She had one hand under her stomach as if she were holding it up, as though it might fall if she let go.

"What is it?" I asked.

"I think I'm in labour," she said.

This was new. She was still late, we were used to that, but a week late felt like she was coming early (James is our only kid who actually arrived on time). It was early in the morning. Around three. From then on, we monitored Jill's contractions, which moved at a crawl, getting closer together as if they were two shy kids at a high-school dance. Things were calm enough when it was time for school that Emily, Cole, and Anna got on the bus. They left the house, and the midwives came in in exchange for our kids, along with our neighbour Gloria, who documented the journey.

We have a photo album from that day. It's a story that belongs in the family of sequential art, along with comics and graphic novels, manga, and wall paintings. The story moves, in images, from left to right, top to bottom. From the start of the album until the last page, it tells the story of Lauren's arrival, right until the moment she emerged from the water into the open air, in one of the best pictures I've ever seen. Unlike Anna, who was born in our bed, Lauren was born in a large bathtub in the bathroom just to the right as you walk inside the house. It's a weird place to have a whirlpool tub, but it was convenient for Lauren's birth. It was big enough to fit two people; I got into the water with Jill and sat behind her while she turned into a superhero and gave birth to our daughter sometime in the early afternoon.

The kids were thrilled to get a new sister. One of the best things about having a baby, if you have other children, is watching them interact with your newborn. We had a parade of visitors who came and spent time with us over the course of the day and throughout the week. My parents, Jill's parents, siblings, neighbours, friends. Everybody was thrilled to have Lauren in our lives; some people even got to hold her when Jill put her down (Jill doesn't let go of her babies often or easily). But there was one person missing, which seems impossible, given how many people came to see our new daughter. A little over two hundred kilometres away, in the city of Brandon, Grandma was in the hospital and in no condition to see Lauren. So, we did the next best thing and brought Lauren to Grandma. We picked the best photograph of Lauren that Gloria had taken, sent it to Walmart in Brandon to be developed, and Jill's grandmother (we call her OGG) brought it to the hospital, to Grandma. I never saw her there. I never saw her after our family visit in Melita. But I know that Grandma had Lauren's picture beside her hospital bed, and knowing that, even today, gives me great comfort.

Relatively soon after Lauren's birth, I spoke with Mom on the phone. She was in Brandon, staying at a hotel near the hospital to be close to Grandma. Uncle Rob was staying in the same hotel. Uncle Rob was with my mom in the hotel room when I spoke to her. They were having a drink, and they both sounded elated and relieved. Given my grandmother's condition, I didn't understand why at first, but quickly learned that Grandma had had a good day, and at that point, a good day was worth celebrating. I didn't quite know what a good day meant, but I opted to think it was an indication that my grandmother would somehow get better; that I'd be able to visit her in Melita during the summer months still and eat buns from the bakery with melted cheese on top; that she'd let me take out Grandpa's truck and drive it around town and through the backroads; that we'd eat supper at the Chicken Chef when we didn't feel like eating at home; that I'd be able to sneak food from the deep freeze at the back of the storage room, right beside Grandpa's old workbench; that I'd write poetry with Grandpa's electric typewriter at the desk in the room I slept in; that Shayne would tell me stories I was never sure were real; we'd golf with Auntie Joan, watch her drop a lit cigarette on the grass in the tee box while she hit her drive, then pick it up and stick it back into her mouth while complaining about the ball she'd just hit; that I'd be able to do all the things I used to, that I hadn't thought I'd get to do again, and everything would be just like it was, and it always would be. We want our families to be immortal, don't we? We hope for the most irrational things and convince ourselves that these things are possible, even probable. Mom and Uncle Rob having drinks at the hotel after spending time with a stronger Grandma could only mean that she'd be discharged and back home soon, taking the picture of Lauren with her to put on her bedside table.

But that's not what happens. That's not what happened.

There's a very real phenomenon called an end-of-life rally, where dying people become more stable, and their decline stops as suddenly and as unexpectedly as Grandma's sickness had started. They're more lucid. They want to eat and drink more, or even at all. They want to visit. And for loved ones who have been prepared to see something entirely different for end-of-life stuff, the rally can be deceptive and confusing.

I think that's what happened with Grandma, as her final decline happened soon after that night, although that's just conjecture. At some point, she was transferred back to Melita Health Centre, and I wasn't able to visit her before she passed. It's one of those decisions I'll regret until I'm as old as she was. I have the same regret with Grandpa. And I would come to have the same regret with my father almost a decade later.

I remember where I was when I heard that Grandma died. There are few things with a stronger tie to place than the news of somebody's death, either a family member or a celebrity. Death, as much as most people fear and hate it, gives meaning and importance to both time and place. For me, the big ones leave a mark as deep and indelible as music. Thinking of the space shuttle *Challenger* will transport me to the living room of my house on Queenston Street when I was nine years old; I was in a canoe with a girlfriend when we learned about Princess Diana; I was in my in-laws' living room when the news flashed about Kobe Bryant, and we all thought it was a prank. These are moments that I will never forget, no matter how old I am. When my grandfather died, my mother brought us all down to the family room in the basement and told us. We hugged like football players in a huddle. When my grandmother died, it was my mother who told me. She called me in the evening, and I remember seeing her number and sensing that something wasn't right, that she wasn't calling for anything good. I didn't want to answer the phone due to that gut feeling, but I did. Jill was with me. We were sitting on the bed together in our bedroom. I collapsed into her arms, and she held me there. It's funny. No matter how much we know death is coming—for everybody, yes, but imminently, for some—it's almost always a shock. For a moment, it takes everything away from you, your words, your breath, and all you can do is hold on to something, like your wife, as if you might fall into the abyss right behind your loved one.

"At least she saw a picture of Lauren."

The funeral was in Melita, and in short order, the family packed and got ready for the trip. It wasn't a long drive, but nobody wanted to sleep in the hotel in town, so we decided to stay in Brandon for the night and then drive the rest of the way for the funeral the following day. When we got to the hotel, I realized that while I had brought my suit, I had forgotten to bring dress shoes. I drove over to the Shoppers Mall on 18th Street and found a place to grab some cheap but passable black dress shoes. Walking back to my car, I felt an odd twinge in my body. I didn't know how to define it. I'd never felt anything like it before. Out of nowhere, I started to feel what I can only describe as weird or off. It was as though I'd stayed up all night, or had a long nap in the middle of the day and had just woken up. Every step I took felt as if I were trudging through thick mud. My skin had pins and needles, like when you sleep on your arm and you wake up to find it dead, and then the feeling starts to come back. Even my vision wasn't right, as if I'd put on a pair of glasses that weren't mine, that had the wrong prescription. The way I saw things when I was a kid walking around the house in the middle of the night was how I saw things that day, walking through the mall towards the parking lot. When I returned to the hotel, still feeling the same way, I told Jill, and she was pragmatic. My grandmother had died. Of course I was going to feel weird. I'd not been eating properly. I'd not been sleeping well. And we were staying in a hotel, waiting to drive to Melita for her funeral. Forgetting my shoes had only compounded the stress. Ironically, it would have been weird if I *didn't* feel weird. It made sense. I did my best to shrug it off.

The memory of my grandmother's interment is clear. The cemetery is beside the Melita Golf Club, closest to the sixth hole. Grandpa is buried there. I used to visit him when I travelled to the community to visit Grandma. Whenever I went there, I would also look for the grave of my grandparents' dog, who died when I was young. Grandpa buried him in the cemetery, along the perimeter fence, and marked the grave with a cross made from sticks. When the cross vanished, so did the grave. Grandpa had a plot beside his that was for Grandma. I always thought of the certainty of that, how there was no question that she would be with him one day. Both in a burial urn. Both ash, as though trying to emulate the soil that surrounded them. His gravestone, their gravestone, I suppose, reads: *TO LIVE IN HEARTS WE LEAVE BEHIND IS*

NOT TO DIE. It reminds me of something Keanu Reeves said when Stephen Colbert, a devout Catholic, asked him what he thought happened when people died. Reeves said, "I know that the ones who love us will miss us." I don't know what I think happens after we die; I think the fear I hold is partially because, deep down, I'm not sure anything happens. But I try to take comfort in the concept of legacy, which is what's being referred to here, really; that leaving something behind with others, a memory or an act or something significant, is good enough. Given the certainty of leaving this world, no matter what anybody believes, I suppose it must be. As a young man, that made me angry, that I'd no choice in the matter. Today, I don't know. You change over the years. Time may provide room for acceptance, but don't we all want more of it? My grandpa's name is on the headstone, above the quote. The headstone is shaped like an open book. On the left-side page of the book was Grandpa's name, Maxwell Eyers, and the date of his birth and death. For thirteen years, Grandma's name, Kathleen Eyers, and her date of birth had been chiselled into the marble on the right-side page. Her date of death is there now. June 26, 2010.

At the interment, there was a small gathering of immediate family. Auntie Joan, my cousin Shayne, Mike and Cam, Mom and Dad, the reverend. Her burial urn was suspended over a small grave pit. After having an initial cry into Jill's shoulder after Mom had called to inform me of Grandma's death, I'd not shed a tear. I'd tried to, not in a performative way but rather because I felt she deserved my tears, and I loved her dearly. Not many people loved watching Tiger Woods with me on a Sunday at a major as much as my grandmother did. I've never, even today, heard a laugh like hers. The next-best laugh in the world belongs to Eden Robinson. They kind of laugh the same, although Eden is louder (in a good way; her joy is contagious). I'll never again eat cheese buns with her at the dining room table. Or see her standing on the driveway waving goodbye until we're completely out of sight, just in case we looked back to see her. I crouched beside the burial urn and placed my hand on it, and that kick-started an onslaught of tears. Cam hugged me, Mike joined in, and that day is now all about loss and coming together.

That summer, I'd started playing ultimate frisbee again, the first time I'd played competitively since the night I was cardio-verted at Seven Oaks General Hospital. It was a co-ed team in one of the lower divisions, but I'd been having fun throwing the disc again, and the team was doing well. We played one of the last games of the regular season a little more than a month after Grandma died. During that time, I'd had spells of feeling off, like I'd felt in the mall in Brandon before my grandmother's funeral. I thought I might have a flu that was stubbornly hanging around, but I brushed the idea off rather quickly as nobody else in my family had gotten sick. I didn't worry much about it, though. It just lingered like an unwanted house guest.

Driving to the game that day, I felt worse than I had before, but when we started playing, the physical activity distracted me from my bodily sensations. Distracted me enough that I had one of my best games of the season. We were playing a team that was higher in the standings than us, but we managed to keep it close. As the game wore on and the points piled up, them scoring a point and then us scoring a point, I spent more time on the sidelines. I felt so bad by the second half that nothing could have distracted me from how I was feeling. Out of it. Disassociated. Tingly. Weak. Shaky. So many symptoms were piling up that I began to change my mind about the flu. I *had* to be sick. There was no other explanation. Near the end of the game, with both teams neck and neck, I sucked it up and got back onto the field, despite feeling like I might fall over. I'm not trying to brag, but I felt a little bit like Michael Jordan clutching it out during the infamous flu game when I contributed to the last few scores and helped my team pull off the upset. After the game, even though everybody was in a celebratory mood, I left quickly. I pulled off my cleats, slipped on my sandals, grabbed my disc, and got into my car. I drove home feeling like I might pass out at any second. It was only then, left to my thoughts with no distractions to speak of, that I began to worry.

When I got home, I went directly to our bedroom and collapsed dramatically onto the bed. I didn't care that Jill was already in there visiting with our neighbour, Tina. In the same breath, I told Jill about the game and that I wasn't feeling right. She asked me how I wasn't feeling right.

I've never known how to describe what anxiety does to my body. I don't think I've ever done it justice (speaking as though it might be offended that I've not acknowledged its physical and mental impact on me properly). What I told Jill that day is how I often express it, for lack of a better explanation as to why I can't get out of bed, why I can't go for a walk, why I can't do any number of things anxiety and its symptoms have prevented me from doing over the years: I don't feel right. I feel like I have a bad flu. I feel unsettled, like my whole body is weak and trembling and ready to break. It's frustrating. I want people to know exactly what I feel, but I do not want them to feel it. It's hard, if not impossible, to appreciate how bad it is unless you feel it, too. It's like in *The Green Mile* when John Coffey takes people's pain away and experiences it, holds it, before releasing it by spitting it out in the form of locusts. That's one of the reasons why dealing with mental health and all its afflictions, from anxiety to depression to everything else, is such an incredibly lonely and isolating feeling. If nobody can understand it, you're on an island, folks.

I'm not sure I did much else that night besides lying in bed thinking. Although I'd felt this way off and on since Grandma's death, I must've now, certainly, come down with a virus. And maybe it was the sort of virus that came in waves, that behaved like my body had been behaving. If that were the case, it was likely that in the morning, I'd wake up feeling just fine and could go about my business. And hopefully, since the mysterious ailment had never felt worse, it had worked its way out of my system. I wouldn't have to deal with it again.

No such luck. When I woke up the next day, I felt worse. And from there, day after day, the feeling in my body, those awful sensations, gathered momentum. I didn't think there was anything

I could do about it. If it was a virus, I would have to wait it out. There is no cure for such an affliction; you get sick and stay sick until you're not sick. This was in July. I saw my family doctor on a particularly hot day during that month. I'd bussed there, and because I had no change to bus home, I had to walk. The doctor had seen me, taken my blood pressure, and done all the obligatory things he had to do to make sure nothing was obviously wrong, and nothing was. To be sure, he sent me to get my blood taken to test my iron level, for diabetes, and many other possible causes. Diabetes runs in my family, on my father's side, and it would've accounted for much of what was going on. I've been tested for it previously but had never tested positive, and I didn't that day either. I made it most of the way home in the heat, wearing pants and an undershirt, having taken off my collared shirt earlier in the more than three-kilometre journey. I took Portage Avenue to Banning, then turned up Banning to get home. I made it a block down Banning before a wave of the now-familiar sensations washed over me. Weakness. Shakiness. Light-headedness. Tingling. Buckling knees. A cold sweat. Spots in my vision. I was only a few minutes from home, but I didn't feel like I could go a step farther. Jill had to come get me with the car and take me home in the middle of making supper. I ate on the couch, half sitting up and half lying down, before moving upstairs to the safety of my bed. I stayed there until morning while Jill and the kids went out and did something fun. I missed out on a lot of things back then, and I've missed out on a lot of things since because of my anxiety.

I continued to go to work, but I did only the bare minimum. This was in the early days of my employment with Workplace

Education Manitoba, running an Indigenous workforce development program in the manufacturing industry. I used the excuse that I was getting acclimated in the first few months of a job, so I didn't have to show much of my progress, just that I'd been reading, researching, and planning. Like Dad, who had an aptitude for program development, I was able to conceptualize a structure for how the initiative would work, and I put some of that down on paper. The difference between me and Dad at that time was that he'd worked hard for his entire life, and I spent most of my time playing solitaire, just trying to get through the days. For breaks, I'd go outside. I worked off Waverley in a mostly industrial area. There was a park across the street and a block away, but that felt too far for me to go, with how weak my legs were, so while outside, within the safe confines of the parking lot, I balanced on parking stops. Going back and forth over the length of the stops served as a distraction, as much as solitaire did. Working would likely have accomplished the same thing, but I couldn't concentrate long enough to do much of that. My mind was too preoccupied with my body; I spent every second of every day, no matter what I was doing, working or not, in bed or up, scanning my body. How was I feeling? Better or worse? Was anything different? Why was it different? Could I breathe in all the way? How far could I breathe in? How long could I hold my breath? How long could the average person hold their breath? It was non-stop.

Workplace Education Manitoba ran programming to develop essential skills that allowed people to function more effectively in the workplace. They ran a regular evening class, and in early August, I attended one of them to assist the facilitator. Getting through the hour that I was there felt as if it were impossible. The countless symptoms I was feeling, the endless sensations trapped within my body, had built to a fever pitch. They were all ramming against one another, screaming for release, and on the way home in the car, after forcing myself to act normal for too long for the benefit of the class, everything exploded all at once. I felt so unbelievably awful that, despite being desperate to get into my bed, I stopped at Shoppers Drug Mart on Portage by Banning Street. I stumbled, probably appearing drunk, to the back of the store, and found the health station where you could take your blood pressure. I slipped my arm into the contraption, pressed start, and the pressure cuff inflated. Several seconds later, the cuff sighed and let go of its grip on my bicep, and the machine provided a reading.

Back then, the health centres at Shoppers locations spat out a reading on a paper slip. I was alarmed by the reading and took the slip with me to show Jill when I got home. The fact that she was concerned enough to tell me to call Health Links scared me, which, in turn, almost certainly jacked up my blood pressure even more. I love nurses. I think they don't get paid enough and don't get enough credit for how hard they work and the kind of work they do. What I have found, however, as they are likely erring on the side of caution, is that when you call Health Links for certain things (e.g., heart issues), they will advise you to call an ambulance. I'd worked myself up into what I now know was my first real panic attack, complete with sweating, chest pressure, elevated heart rate *and* blood pressure, and a pounding heart—all the hallmarks of a panic attack and, incidentally, a heart attack. I called 9–1–1 and told them what was going on, and they dispatched an ambulance to my house. It was the first of two times I would call an ambulance that year.

While we waited for the ambulance, Jill got on the phone with family—my mom and her mom—to tell them what was happening. We were both scared. I'd never seen Jill scared like that. Whatever buildup there had been, whatever indications there were that something like this was going to happen, and the clues that pointed to this being a panic attack and not heart-related (the fact that I had already dealt with a heart issue contributed to the concern), the eruption of it, the suddenness of how bad it got, left no room for any rational thought. Now that I am years removed from that moment, I can be objective about it, and I know that not only was that my first panic attack, but it was also when I had a nervous breakdown. It's unquestionable. The move, the job change, the new baby, the death of my grandmother. We're all human, and we can only take so much. We have an internal threshold, how much we can take, and when that threshold is exceeded, you get something like what happened to me. Your body and your mind put their hands on your cheeks, stare you right in the eye so that you pay attention—because you haven't been paying attention to the signs, you haven't been taking care of yourself properly, you've let yourself get to this point—and say, "You are fucking done. If you won't wake up, we will do it for you."

Breakdown.

FIVE
STANDING IN A MOMENT

Paramedics checked my vitals and asked me what was going on. I recounted everything as best I could, and then, with some help, I walked downstairs to the first floor and outside into the front yard. That took a lot out of me. There were days I didn't think I could make it across the hallway to the bathroom because I was sure my legs would give out, that I'd collapse. I use my words carefully when I talk or write about what I feel I can't do. I'm deliberate in using "I felt like I couldn't" or "I didn't think that I could," because the reality was that I could have, and often, despite what I believed I was incapable of, I did. But the idea that something awful would happen to me if I tried, usually death, built my anxiety up until it was bigger than me. I didn't know back then that my knees felt like they would buckle because I was carrying all that weight.

Standing in place, stuck in a moment, unable to escape it.

The paramedics helped me onto a gurney in the front yard. Some of our neighbours had come to see what was happening; it's always unsettling when there's an ambulance on your block. They encouraged me as I was loaded into the ambulance. I didn't understand why then, but I felt safe and less panicked when I was in the vehicle surrounded by medical professionals. That ought to have been an indication to me that something not entirely physical was going on. That didn't mean my physical symptoms weren't real; it meant that the cause was not what I thought; that is, a heart attack. If that wasn't a clue, the fact that we were driving without lights and sirens should have been. Even though the paramedics were great, and I was well cared for, there wasn't a huge rush to get me to the hospital; they, along with the doctors I eventually saw, likely had a good idea of what was happening. I am sure it wasn't the first time they'd been called to the home of somebody suffering from a strong panic attack.

Let me get this out of the way. I feel a lot of shame and regret not only for that ambulance ride to the hospital but the one I would take less than two months later, and all the other times I've gone to the emergency room when I didn't have to. I don't like to think that I've been a strain on the health-care system, but I know that I have been. Almost every single time that I have gone to the hospital because of a panic attack, or an irregular heartbeat, or whatever else was going on inside my body, I have been sent home without any further treatment, save the provision of anti-anxiety medication, and often with the advice that I should make an appointment with my doctor. There are only two exceptions. The first was when Dan took me to Seven Oaks because of my SVT, and I was cardioverted. The second was when the van hit me. Other than that, I could have stayed home instead of going to Emergency via ambulance or under my own power.

I'm not going to say that I would have been fine, or even okay, because I wasn't fine, but I would have lived. Knowing this, being acutely aware of it, sometimes changes nothing.

As far as I've come in my journey with mental health, I'm intimately aware that it's a journey with no finish line, and one that often has wrong turns that lead you back to a place you've already been. Two steps forward, one step back. Just last month, I was having some heart issues (that were certainly exacerbated by stress, being overtired, and resultant anxiety), and my knee-jerk reaction was to get in the car and drive to Grace Hospital, which I did. Six hours later, without any medical treatment, just some tests, I was on my way home, having wasted a large chunk of my day and having been absent from the house and my wife and kids. But that's why it's a sickness. That's why it's a lifelong thing. There will always be setbacks. There is no cure. You have to try to keep growing and learn how to live with what you've got a little more effectively each day. Sometimes you do, and sometimes you don't, and that's okay. You cannot beat yourself up over your perceived failures.

At the hospital, I lay in the waiting room on a gurney, as if on display, for several hours until they had a bed for me. While I was waiting with one of the paramedics who brought me in (evidently, they have to stay with you until you're moved to a bed), a nurse came and took my blood. By the time I'd switched from the gurney to a bed, the results had returned and showed that whatever they'd tested for was normal. The ECG was normal, too.

Everything was normal. As far as anybody could tell (I would be told this repeatedly for the next several months), I was a healthy young man.

I couldn't accept that. I couldn't believe it. Given the complete anarchy that was going on underneath my skin, there was no way that something wasn't seriously wrong. Nobody healthy, as they said I was, could possibly feel the way I felt—and, again, that's the isolating thing about mental health. You are impartially and demonstrably physically healthy, so how can anybody understand how terrible you feel? They can't.

That paramedic who had to wait with me tried to make conversation, to keep my mind on something else, because he knew I was scared. He probably ended up knowing as much about me as the nurse who was with me when I was on the truth serum. He asked me what I did for a living, about my kids. I told him that I had a new daughter. We discussed what I was up to in August, before autumn set in. In less than two weeks, Jill, the kids, and I were supposed to be headed up to Clear Lake for the week. Ever since I was a kid, with very few exceptions, I'd spent a week every year in Wasagaming, mostly at a resort called Thunderbird Bungalows. I always looked forward to the week; that place holds a lot of memories. When I was sixteen, I went to the bar underneath Pizza Place and didn't get carded. I was with Mike. We got drunk and had to sneak into the cabin late and not get caught by Mom. I think we were successful, but then again, sometimes parents know things and don't bother to say anything. I know I've done that a few times with my kids. As a parent, you learn when to let kids be kids. When I played ultimate, I used to throw the disc with Cam between the cottages. There were park benches, fire pits, a play structure, and these old-fashioned lamps. I threw an errant frisbee one evening and broke the glass on one of the lamps; it stayed broken for years afterwards. We made friends with a family from Saskatchewan. They used to set up their television outside one of the cottages and watch a Roughriders game. Their family was in the wine business and wasn't shy to share drinks with everybody. We went on a hike near the lake, got lost, and had to carry kids through deep water. There used to be a Halloween party in Wasagaming where kids dressed up and got candy from all the vendors along Wasagaming Drive. It was supposed to be a kids' thing, but it was mostly for parents. Jill and I, Cam and his family, filled sippy cups with alcohol and drank for the whole walk. By the time we got back to the cottage and sat down to play cards, we were incredibly drunk. Grandma and Grandpa used to stay in a hotel across the back lane from us. Uncle Rob and Aunt Paula, Mom's brother and sister-in-law, came out a few times. One year, they brought their daughter, Alex. She would've been around one. To this day, I swear *Dave* was her first word. I lost my brand-new sunglasses in the middle of the lake while bouncing off waves in a tube being pulled by a pontoon boat. It seemed that every year, new memories were made, but in 2010, that year, I wasn't sure there'd be any memories at all.

"That'll be fun," the paramedic said when I told him about the Clear Lake trip.

"I can't go to Clear Lake," I said. "Not like this."

He swore that I could do it. He said that in a couple of weeks,

I'd be fine. I didn't think it was possible. How would I go to the lake if I wasn't sure I could make it across the hallway or up a flight of stairs? We went to the pool every day and played chicken with the kids. Cam and I had contests to see who could swim the pool length and back while underwater. We walked everywhere, all the time. We did trails like the Ominnick Marsh. I had an annual golf game at Clear Lake Golf Course with Dad and Cam, and sometimes Mike, if he was there. We rarely sat still unless we went to see the bison or hung out together on the dock at Lake Katherine.

My family came to see me in the hospital to check on me, but it felt as if they were saying goodbye to a loved one in hospice care. I was sure that within months, if not weeks, I would be dead. By the time I left the hospital, the sun was coming up. I'd been there all night and was no better leaving than when I'd arrived. All I had to show for my hours in the emergency room was a bracelet with my name, date of birth, and health number on it, a doctor's assurance that I'd only suffered a panic attack, and a bottle of lorazepam.

Until the day before we left for the lake, maybe even on the day we left, I was set on staying home and letting Jill and the kids go. I thought I'd ruin the week. Since the hospital trip, I'd done nothing more than lie around, feel sorry for myself, generally feel awful, and live in fear.

More than ever, doing the smallest task seemed like the biggest obstacle. The only thing I could do, because I *had* to do it, was go to work. But if you're reading this, Kara (my old boss), I'm sorry: I did very little work. Less than ever before. Instead, I spent every second living in my obsession with symptoms that were riding roughshod through every inch of my body. I made a habit of balancing on parking stops, of walking to the end of them and back, endlessly, during breaks. I played solitaire fifty times a day. I ate at my desk, avoiding any small talk I might have to engage in. I prayed to God, if there was one, to take the sickness away from me. In what became a morning ritual and a scene in my book *The Theory of Crows*, I pulled up to work one morning and saw rotten shards of wood from a wing pallet in a peculiar shape. I got out of my car, walked around to the front of it, crouched down, and stared at the crude shape of a cross. I hoped it was a sign. You think and do the most desperate things when you're suffering.

I've never been sure about the existence of God. I've tried hard to believe. When you're certain that you're going to die, when you're terrified at the prospect of eternity, especially eternal darkness, God is a good proposition. So good that it's enough to take Pascal's wager, knowing that you cannot, with certainty, prove the existence of God. So, you bet there is a God regardless of proof because you've got everything to gain and nothing to lose. If you're dead and there's nothing, you're still dead. Oh well.

It's not that I have never experienced something that could be interpreted as supernatural. Things have happened to me that are beyond my ability to explain rationally. I've received a sign from God right when I asked for one. When I worked for MPI, there was a period when Jill and I were struggling financially; it was so hard at times that we didn't have a dime to spare. I had a friend I'd not seen for a long time and stupidly made plans to meet them at lunch one day at one of the hot dog vendors on Broadway Avenue. The problem was that I didn't have enough money for a hot dog. On my walk to work that morning, I was navigating through two options: how to explain why I wasn't eating anything during our lunch date (I thought I might tell him that I was getting over a stomach virus) or cancelling on him until I could afford to buy a hot dog. I'd just crossed Isabel Street, still on Cumberland Avenue, when I said a prayer that went something like this:

"God, I know you've got better things to do than worry about whether or not I have a hot dog for lunch, but if you don't mind, could you please find a way to lend me some money?"

A second after praying, I looked to my right, and folded up neatly on the street, nestled against the curb, was a crisp ten-dollar bill. My prayers had been answered. The kicker was that my friend treated me, so I didn't need the ten dollars after all.

That morning, with my car pulled up so close that my front bumper almost touched the rotten wood shaped into a cross, I knelt, put my hand on the wood, closed my eyes, and prayed for all the hurt and chaos and fear to be taken away from me. I prayed for health. I didn't care about money or material things. I just wanted to wake up in the morning and feel human again. That's it.

The following day, I felt the same way I had every morning for the past few months.

My fear ran so deep, was so out of control, that I was too scared to take medication designed to alleviate the symptoms of anxiety. I was lying down in Cole's bed one evening when my father came over to see me. He sat at the edge of my bed, talked to me, and listened to me. I was crying most of the time. I told him that I felt so weak, so unsteady. The pills I'd been given were on the floor beside the bed. Dad picked up the bottle and asked me what they were, and I told him. I told him how scared I was to take them. I had read everything about the medication, including the possible side effects, the likely ones and the rare ones. Dizziness. Restlessness. Memory loss. Confusion. Blurred vision. Seizures. Drowsiness. Irritability. Anxiety. Anxiety! Like I needed more of that. And how could they cause restlessness and drowsiness simultaneously? What kind of meds were these? He opened the bottle, asked me to open my mouth, which I did, and placed a little blue pill on my tongue. It could have worked. It could have been my father's presence that made me feel slightly calmer for a little while. It's funny. Even now, I'm more apt to believe it was my father rather than the drug, even though I have found that specific medication works for me.

That was the only time I'd taken lorazepam when I wasn't in a hospital emergency room (I'd gotten a few big doses of the medication in the middle of the panic attacks I mistook for heart attacks). I took the bottle of little blue pills with me to Wasagaming, thinking that if things got bad, I would take one, but I never did, which is not to say that things weren't bad; it was just that they never got to the point where I needed to call an ambulance. I had no panic attacks, just the persistent, pervasive sensations in my body and the constant fear in my mind. I held the bottle of little blue pills when a blood doctor called me back to make an appointment. By then, I'd been dealing with symptoms long enough that I was willing to try everything and anything except anti-anxiety medication, and I'm not sure why. The best answer I can give is that I felt like I'd be weak if I took drugs. I never understood, as I do now, that mental illness is an illness, and sometimes, when you have an illness, you need medication for it. You aren't a failure if you take cough syrup when you have a cough, so you aren't a failure if you take anti-anxiety medication when you have anxiety; it's just that there are other things you can do in concert with a drug regimen to eliminate the need for drugs over the long-term (something that I've not been successful with yet).

We knew somebody who'd seen a blood doctor, and like a psychic (probably exactly like a psychic), they were able to get a lot of information just by looking at a drop of blood on a slide under a microscope. The problem was that the blood doctor couldn't see me for a few months. On the phone, pacing the cabin, I agreed to the appointment, but in my mind, I didn't think there was any chance I'd live that long. I made it to see the blood doctor, whose office was somewhere outside city limits. It was odd. She knew things about me from looking at a drop of my blood that I didn't think she could know, but I think that's what people say about psychics and other such professions. I remember her saying, "You're a healthy man, David," and I allowed myself to feel relieved by that, if only for a few hours. She knew that I didn't sleep well and that I was tired often. I looked at Jill like, *Holy shit, she knows that I have trouble sleeping!* but anybody would have looked at me back then and known I wasn't sleeping; all you had to do was see the bags under my eyes, the messy hair because I never bothered combing it, the constant yawning, the lack of colour in my face. The treatment I was given was an armful of expensive vitamins and supplements. I think I took as many vitamins as I did lorazepam.

Jill didn't think I should go to Clear Lake that year, and in hindsight, she was right. She usually is, as much as I hate to admit it sometimes, because I think I should win more arguments than I do. Given the way I was feeling, and how the way I was feeling was controlling my behaviour and ability to engage with others, she thought that if I went I would put a strain on the week that the kids, more than anybody, didn't need. That's exactly what happened, but two things convinced me to go, in my messed-up way of thinking. First, if Jill and the kids went and I stayed home, what would I do if something happened to me and I was alone? Jill would come home from the lake, and she'd find a cold, dead body. Second, though I'd been unable to do it yet, I thought I could mask what was going on with me. I could tough it out for a week and do things that Jill and I both thought I could not do (I didn't think I was physically capable of doing things; Jill knew I was physically capable but didn't think I could overcome my fear).

For most of the week, I was a burden, and it left Jill having to do almost everything from the moment we arrived. While she and the big kids unloaded the car and got the cabin set up, I lay on the couch like some lazy asshole and watched golf. There were moments when things *almost* felt normal, when whatever I was doing fleetingly distracted me from my body. I went to the pool a couple of times with the kids and even got in the water. I liked being in the water. There was something about being in the cold that seemed to numb out the symptoms. There's a picture of Cam and me in the pool where, if you didn't know any better, you'd think I was perfectly healthy. Not a care in the world. There's a picture of me on a lawn chair, the one my dad used to sit on all the time, with Lauren, who was just two months old, in my lap. She's resting against my legs, looking at me. I'm turned away, towards the camera, a forced smile on my face. People might think it's a good picture. A cute picture. Jill and I know better. I felt awful. My hair hadn't been combed for weeks. I'd not showered in forever. I guess what's important is that Lauren, when she sees that picture, doesn't know. She just sees her dad holding her, and I like that. I like it, but I know it's an illusion. I was present, but I was not, and that kills me.

Dad told me that there's no point in regretting anything, because you can't change what's happened. But there are so many things I'd do differently if I could. I was sure that any false move could mean my death, but it wouldn't have. That week. Those months. That year. These years. It could've all been so different if only I'd known then what I know now. The bad outweighed the good that week in August 2010, no matter how many pictures deceptively say otherwise. I shouldn't have gone, but I went. And I came back feeling worse than ever. I came back stuck in a moment I didn't believe I'd get out of, sinking in quicksand but not struggling, as though resigned to my fate. It shows how terrible things were inside that body of mine that I was giving up, succumbing to the fear, right when one of my dreams was finally about to come true: my first published book was coming out.

I ruined that as well.

I've wanted to be a writer since I was in the third grade. It's funny to think of how young I was, because you have to wonder if it's possible to be certain about your life when you're eight. Of my five kids, my youngest, James, is eight. He seems so young. I look at him occasionally and think about how I was his age, exactly, when I decided what I wanted to do when I grew up. I wonder if what he's doing now is something he'll be doing for his career. Then I get scared, because presently, he cares about one thing and one thing only: being a goalie. A hockey goalie, to be precise. You know, with the equipment that costs thousands of dollars, that he'll grow out of every year until he stops growing, oh, about one thousand years from now. If he sticks with it, I'm going to be buying goalie equipment for a decade, and with every book that comes out, I pray it will do well so that I can support my son's dreams. But will that dream stick? Mine did. The moment I finished my first book, a work of poetry entitled *The Bestest Poems I've Ever Sawed*, and my teacher made it into a saddle-stitched booklet, there was nothing I wanted more in the world than to write books.

It took a long time for that dream to be realized. I tell new and emerging writers that if you write, you're a writer. But being a published author is something different. It's hard to break into the publishing industry. You control some things, and other things come down to luck. The argument can be made that, to some extent, you make your own luck, but luck plays into it all the same. You're in control of how hard you're willing to work. I'm not the most talented writer out there, but I want to be, and I work hard at getting there. I've tried all different forms and genres, and it's helped me to develop skills and voice. I write a lot, so I don't read as much as I should, but I do read (I call it targeted reading); the more you read, the better you'll write. And you have to have something to say; you have to tap into your passion and share that passion through Story. People always say, "Write what you know," but writing is an act of exploration, self-reflection, and personal growth. I can say that more now than ever, in writing this story. If you only write what you know, how are you growing? Instead, write to your passion, write what you want to know, write to understand, write to connect, but don't stay hidden in your comfort zone (an ironic thing for somebody with anxiety to say, I know). When you write about something you're passionate for, you connect with people who feel that passion, or share it.

That's what led me to write comics; I wanted to undo the harm that the comics I read as a boy did by creating comics with positive representation and real history. I started with *The Life of Helen Betty Osborne* and, through hard work and luck, created an opportunity to write more for Portage & Main Press and, eventually, its Indigenous literature imprint, HighWater Press. The first graphic novel I wrote for them was called *7 Generations*, and it came out over a series of four issues—*Stone, Scars, Ends/Begins*, and *The Pact*. I dug in and finished multiple scripts over a short period. Scott Henderson, my illustrator, dug in, too, pen-

cilling and inking the pages efficiently without sacrificing quality. Once we had two books out and available to purchase, my
first launch was scheduled for fall 2010. When the date was set
for the book launch, I hadn't yet had a breakdown. But with the
October launch date fast approaching, something I'd been looking forward to, dreaming of, for decades became an event that I
couldn't imagine doing. I allowed my anxiety, my mental health
illness, to steal the joy from a fulfilled dream, and with little to
no resistance.

The launch was at McNally Robinson Booksellers, in the
Prairie Ink Restaurant, at 7:00 p.m.: the best time and the best
place to have a book launch in the city. I went with Jill, and when
we pulled up to the bookstore, I could see that the place was already filling up. The biggest fear an author has before an event is
almost always over whether anybody will show up. Sometimes,
you never know. Even deep into my career, as an established author and presumably with some following, I've had the odd event
where almost nobody has come. It has to do with timing; it has to
do with location; it has to do with weather—several factors com-
bine to create a perfect storm of empty seats. This was not one of
those events. I could tell the place was going to be packed, but as
Jill and I walked towards the front door, I felt like I might fall over.
The non-stop anxiety I'd been suffering with since July was amp-
ing up at the worst possible time, rushing from bad to worse. We
took a detour and used the mall entrance beside the bookstore
rather than the entrance to the bookstore itself, opting to sit on a
bench in the mall. I was crying. I was telling Jill that I wanted to
go home. There was no way that I'd be able to stand long enough

to take part in the launch. Wasn't that what I had to do? Stand at a podium for a long time and talk about the book, read from it, take questions, and then, after all that torture, sit and sign books and talk to people. The launch was supposed to be an hour, and I didn't think I'd be able to make it through five minutes.

After Clear Lake, nothing had improved. It was in September that I'd called for my second ambulance ride to the emergency room. Cole, my oldest son, was getting into hockey; he'd just turned five years old. We put him in a camp in early September, leading up to the start of the hockey season. He was going to play Timbits that year. The camp was at Canlan Sports, on Ellice Avenue near the airport. I had to drop him off in the morning and pick him up later in the day. It combined hockey, dryland training (like soccer), and lunch between activities. As parents do when their kids are very young, I dropped Cole off for his camp fully dressed in his hockey equipment, so all I had to do when he got into the locker room was put on his helmet and tie his skates.

It was a lot for me to do first thing in the morning, and I still had to get to work. I'd not slept well again the night before. I'd not been sleeping well for quite some time. When your nerves are fried, it's hard to settle your body and mind down enough to rest. I'd been prescribed sleeping pills but didn't want to take them. There were a few nights when I didn't sleep at all. I had what Google told me was *terminal insomnia.* You can fall asleep, but then, in the night, you wake up. It could be three in the morning; it could be one in the morning. Whenever you wake up, you can't go back to sleep. Typically, I woke up around one; I'd lie in bed wide awake until sunrise and it was time to get out of bed. Sleeping well is essential to fight against anxiety. Conversely, being overtired puts out the welcome mat. I was exhausted all the time, and that morning I dropped Cole off at hockey camp was no different.

Cole's skates were dull, so I had to get them sharpened in the pro shop at the front of the building. We made it inside and I gave Cole's skates to the kid working the desk with no problem, but as I walked out, without any warning except for a quiver that rolled over my body, my heart started to pound. It wasn't beating fast. It wasn't like another episode of SVT years after it had been corrected. My heart was jackhammering as if there were somebody inside my chest beating the hell out of my ribs. I'd never felt anything like it before. In the months that I'd felt too many symptoms to count, this one was new. I don't think I've felt my heart thump like that since. I walked out of the pro shop with my hand against the wall to steady myself, having lost sight of everything but myself. I forgot that Cole was standing with me, probably terrified when he saw his father put his back against the wall beside the front office window and slide down onto the floor. I heard his voice, but I didn't answer him. I was too busy calling 9–1–1. Again. I told the operator what was happening, and they dispatched an ambulance to Canlan. Sometime between when the ambulance was sent and when it arrived, I told Jill what was happening, and somebody came to watch Cole like I should have been doing. When the ambulance came, they helped me onto the stretcher inside, wheeled me out, and then drove away to the hospital, leaving behind my son and whoever had come to help him with his skates and helmet.

I abandoned my son. For the longest time, I never considered how scared he must have been. I never considered how he could play hockey and soccer and eat lunch that day without worrying about his dad. Cole's resilient, he always has been, but he was still just a kid, and I left him there, too involved in myself to even look at him, to comfort him and let him know that everything was okay. In my eyes, when I recall those months, the worst months of my life—at least until a decade later—that moment was my rock bottom. Your first concern when you have kids is their well-being. That comes before everything, especially yourself. You think of them before you think of you. You are present for them, and when you have a chance to tell them not to be afraid, so they can be kids and not worry, you tell them, even if you don't think things are going to be okay. It's not fair to put something like that on a child. I wasn't fair to Cole, and during those months, during the last fourteen years, I've not been fair to my family on too many occasions to count.

I want to think I've gotten better as time has gone by, but my deepest fear is that I've not been the father they deserve. They've seen me go through this anxiety and this depression with so much fear, and I don't know what that's taught them. Even now, they go on hikes with Jill or somewhere fun that requires a fraction of physical activity, and I stay home. They don't expect me to come anymore. You don't get that time back. I don't know what that says about me or how that makes them think about me. I want them to feel like, to *know*, they matter to me more than anything, more than fear, because they do. So, what's my problem? And for what? By the time Cole was done at camp for the day, I was leaving the emergency room with another new bracelet and my system numbed by lorazepam.

There was no choice at the launch. I couldn't leave and go home. People were there, waiting for the event to start. Everything was set up. As it got closer to 7:00 p.m., I knew that Scott Henderson, the illustrator, would be in the store, along with my publisher, HighWater Press. Scott's mom and Angela, his wife at the time. My parents. My family. All I could do was calm myself as much as possible, at least enough to get me through the hour. After that, it didn't matter. I could cry all the way home; I could cry and shake all the way to my bed, where I spent most of my time when I wasn't at work playing solitaire in my cubicle. Jill got me a bottle of orange juice from the store down the hall. I probably hadn't eaten or drank much that day, and in a pinch, it would give me a bit of energy. Eventually, it was time; there could be no more stalling. Jill helped me to my feet, and we walked to the bookstore's mall entrance. I did what I'd done at work before entering the building every morning and put on a face, a plastic face, a mask that would fool everybody into thinking everything was just fine. That I was just fine. That there was no war raging inside my body, no thoughts so heavy it felt as if they'd crush me. That I was steady and strong.

If there are pictures of me from the book launch, you would not be able to tell that I was suffering from severe anxiety, that I was in the middle of a nervous breakdown, that I'd lost a ton of weight, that I'd spent countless hours in bed, leaving my wife to do all the work, to live life with the kids because I was not prepared to risk staying on my feet any longer than I had to. You would think that I looked just like anybody else, that I was a young author launching his first book, and that my dream of being a writer had come true. Maybe I was a bit nervous, but who wouldn't be?

Though the launch itself is a blur, when I was at the podium, talking about the book and answering questions, I likely didn't notice my anxiety as much as usual. I've always been weird like that. Many people rank public speaking as something they fear more than death. I can't wrap my head around that. I mean, I get it, but I cannot fathom anything being more terrifying than death. According to the National Institute of Mental Health, 75 percent of people rank public speaking as their number-one fear. Generally, this means speaking to a large audience. The technical term is *glossophobia*, in case you're wondering. *Seventy-five percent*. Most people would rather die than speak in public. I love public speaking, which must sound extremely odd coming from somebody who has terrible anxiety. Quite the opposite of fear, I find public speaking calming. I don't know why, but it's always been the case. Maybe it's because when I'm giving a talk to a large group, it distracts me from what's going on inside my body. Maybe it's because, just like when I was young, I like being the centre of attention. Maybe it's both. All I know is that when I get up in front of a gym full of five hundred kids, it's like going to the spa.

The important thing here, and what I didn't acknowledge

then, is that even though I was positive I couldn't do it; even though I was confident, beyond a shadow of a doubt, that I'd collapse during the launch because I'd not been on my feet for that long since July; even though I cried on the bench in the mall for half an hour before the launch started; and even though all the little monsters were whispering into my ear that I'd fail, that I'd fall, that I'd die if I went into that bookstore and launched my first published books, I fucking did it. And what that should say to you is that when you feel the same way, when you don't think that you can get up in front of a crowd, or walk to the end of the block and back, or you think you have no business working the job you were hired to do, or that you're going to fail at something you've worked hard for, or that you can't walk up the stairs, you can fucking do it, too. Whatever those little monsters are saying to you, they are *always* lying, no matter how convincing they sound.

I put together playlists for my books and listen to them while I write. It gets me in the right frame of mind. It helps me find the passion and inspiration I need to put my best stuff down, or at least put enough good stuff down that my editor can work with it. I've been listening to a lot of Florence + the Machine lately. I don't know why I'm late to the game, but I love that Florence Welch speaks and sings a lot about her anxiety. Sometimes, I hear lyrics that say things better than what I've been trying to say for an entire page.

To exist in the face of suffering and death
And somehow still keep singing

I like that. That's what I'm talking about. I wish I'd had that song fourteen years ago. I wish I'd had that song five years ago. I wish I'd had that song twenty years ago. I wish I'd known then what I know now. I wish I'd never forgotten to somehow still keep singing, even now.

After the launch, with the crowd dispersed and having said my goodbyes to family and friends who had come to support me, I left with a sense of relief, not accomplishment. I didn't feel any better. Nothing had changed. What bothered me, then and now, is that it should've been an amazing night. I should've stayed out and gone to celebrate somewhere. Everything I'd dreamed of had happened. Everything I'd dreamed of was happening *right then*, but all I could do was get into my car with Jill, feel fortunate that I'd not passed out or died during the event, and look forward to being in bed.

Anxiety sucks the joy out of everything. I can't tell you the number of things that have happened since 2010 that I should remember only in a positive way but can't because anxiety was there with me, weighing me down, standing on my shoulders, hogging the spotlight of my memory. Sometimes, my brain mercifully filters the anxiety out, so that even when I'm sure my mental health was at a low point at a given moment, I can't recall the anxiety unless I try to. When James was born, I held him by the window late in the evening under light filtering through the glass in an otherwise dark hospital room and looked at him with disbelief because Jill and I had made a human being. I know I was feeling terrible, but it's like my mind was telling my anxiety, "You can't have this memory." I was marvelling at the beauty of my son sleeping in my arms, but I was terrified that I wouldn't be around to watch him grow up, to be there for him when he needed his dad. In my memory of that night, the fear takes a back seat, but usually, anxiety is front and centre in my recollections. If memories were selfies, anxiety is photobombing a lot of pictures, or it's at my side with its arm around my shoulders, smiling triumphantly while I'm frowning.

I think about that now and consider all the joy anxiety has stolen from me. In those moments when I had these disaster thoughts, when I was catastrophizing, I filled my head with negative emotions, exactly the opposite of what I should have been feeling. Anxiety took away from the reality of the situation. In a way, I lost those moments. They're gone. Anxiety took my book launch away from me. I invited it in to do so. And it doesn't matter that my body felt the way it did. I wasn't imagining that I'd had a nervous breakdown. I felt like shit. My knees were weak. My legs were tired. My heart was heavy. My fingers were tingling. There was pressure on my head. All of that was real. It was happening. But I *chose* to worry about it, and I *chose* to let the worry take over. I almost allowed it to prevent me from taking part in the launch. If it weren't for Jill, I would've gone home. I would've called McNally Robinson and told them that I was sick. I've done something like that before. I've cancelled entire trips where I was going to an event in another city for my books because my anxiety was so bad, and I didn't think I could do it. Stolen joy, stolen moments, stolen time. And what has it given me? Nothing.

That's where depression creeps in. I don't see how it can't. Anxiety opens the door for it. They are friends, you see. Anxiety and depression. In my life, one has led to the other until they both took up residence in my body and my mind. It starts with a tiny thought. Take the time I was at Clear Lake pacing back and forth in the living room in our cabin on the phone with the blood doctor, making an appointment for months down the road, thinking, *I will never live to make that appointment.* There comes a time when that cancerous thought grows into *I don't* want *to live to make that appointment.* Why the change? I cannot imagine living the next ten years the way I am living now, let alone the next forty years. What kind of life would that be, even if I am allowed to keep some memories and forget my anxiety's place in them? It doesn't change the fact that I am feeling what I am feeling at that time, at that moment. It is crushing to believe that your life has become the sum of your anxiety. And because you think that nobody can understand what you're feeling, it's profoundly lonely. And loneliness is a factor in the development of depression.

In the fall and through the early winter of 2010, I sought counselling for the first time from a man whose office was out near the University of Manitoba. He was a good, kind man with a calm demeanour and an aura of empathy and understanding. He was a Christian counsellor, which reminded me of Dad, who was a minister and a trained counsellor. How Dad talked to me during my darkest moments revealed that to me. Sometimes, he talked to me more like a therapist than a father, or rather, he found the balance between the two. He was always about finding balance.

Seeing a Christian counsellor seemed a stretch for me because of my inability to find authentic faith in God. I question too much. That's a product of anxiety, as well. I had Bible verses taped to the inside door of my bedroom closet, and they meant something to me, but it was about the words, not an omniscient entity. "Can any one of you by worrying add a single hour to your life?" That's Matthew 6:27. Whether or not God is real, those words are meaningful. I liked the idea of God. I liked the idea of an afterlife because I was so afraid of there not being one. So afraid of there being only eternal emptiness. My father believed in God, and if he believed in God, there *had* to be something to it. Dad was smart and rational and he wasn't one to put faith into something he wasn't certain was there. Dad told me that he saw Memekwesewak, little people, on the trapline when he was a boy, so I take that as gospel. But there's a nagging thought at the back of my mind no matter how many signs I get, or how much I believe Dad or my wife or the counsellor I tried: If I cannot see or feel God, how can I be sure that God exists? And I was so mad at God, too, if God was there, because I'd prayed a million times for God to take away what was happening to me, and he never lifted a finger. Every day it seemed as though I was only getting worse.

Still, the counsellor I saw was a soft-spoken, thoughtful, smart guy. For the first few sessions I had with him, surprisingly, God didn't factor into our ongoing conversation. I told him about me, about everything I could think of that led up to my nervous breakdown and all that had happened since. I liked seeing him for our weekly sessions because he was a good listener, and sometimes, with anxiety and depression, you need somebody to listen to you non-judgmentally. You need to share what you're going through and have somebody understand, or at least try to understand. He gave me strategies to try that may or may not have been effective, although I never felt much better and never quite crawled out of the hole I was in. One strategy was the tapping method, which I tried a hundred times without any noticeable results. The technical name for it is EFT, or Emotional Freedom Technique.

You tap a certain number of times, in particular places, in a specific sequence. The top of your head. Your inner eyebrows. Under your eyes. Under your nose. And so on. You do it with your index fingers while focusing on a feeling or an issue you want to resolve; it's supposed to reduce anxiety or stress, among other outcomes. The other method was EMDR, or Eye Movement Desensitization and Reprocessing, a process that helps you heal from emotional distress stemming from past trauma. EMDR asks that you move your eyes in a certain way while you process traumatic experiences in your life; doing so removes the fight-or-flight response elicited by them. You remember them, but they have no hold over you. I remember feeling lost when practising EMDR because I had no idea what had caused my nervous breakdown. It was several different things that, once piled on top of each other, caused an explosion that fried my nerves. Because there were four or five events that served as the catalyst for my struggles, I found it impossible to focus on any one of them or to figure out which one had caused more trauma than the other. And some didn't cause trauma at all, like the birth of my daughter—it was just an added stress. And so, even though my first therapist was a lovely man, lovely wasn't cutting it, it wasn't helping me, and the methods he gave me were ineffective (which is not to say that they have not been, or are not, effective for other people; they just weren't for me, for the place I was in). Talking helped me most in those sessions, but even though he listened, I don't think he got it. I don't think he got *me*. After a few sessions, when he brought God into it, suggesting that I was under a spiritual attack, he lost me.

The months from July to January were agonizing, and because I was suffering each and every day, time passed slowly. Seconds felt like minutes. Minutes felt like hours. Hours felt like days. Days felt like weeks. Weeks felt like months. Autumn gave way to winter. The days got shorter, and the nights became longer. And though the seasons changed, as they inevitably do, nothing changed for me. I woke up in the morning, stayed in bed until I had to get up, then ate what I could and went to work. I spent most of the day at my desk, in my cubicle, doing whatever I could muster up the energy to do, but mostly pretending to do more than I was. It was a miracle that I managed to build a program; I wonder what I could have accomplished if I had been able to put everything into it. When I wasn't at my desk, I was balancing on parking stops, even in the winter, because I liked being out in the cold. I convinced myself that numbing my skin helped numb my anxiety. One day, I wrecked the accidental wooden cross in the parking lot out of frustration. After work, I got home, had supper, and got into bed.

Meanwhile, Jill and the kids went about their lives, doing things without me, and it became normal for the kids to see me in bed; I hate more than almost anything else from that time in my life that that was their reality. It wasn't me. I used to be healthy. I used to play basketball every day and come back to work sweating like crazy. I used to go out with friends and have fun, drink, and be stupid. Now if I drank, it was to numb out the anxiety, and I never went out with anybody. I was a recluse. If I was able to have moments of clarity, I'd feel such sadness that the father my kids knew was not the person I really was, the person I really am. Even now, years removed from that time, but still struggling more often than I'd like, I want my kids to know a little bit of a better Dad than they have.

I was always tired. I lost lots of weight. As a result, being that I was progressively weaker and unwilling to do anything about it, my anxiety went unchecked. It grew bigger, I got smaller, and it threatened to swallow me whole. There were times that my fear of death was eclipsed by my fear of living this way for however long I had left. I wasn't quite at that point, but I was getting there much faster than the days were long.

And then Jill changed it all.

I often say when I give public talks, and I give a lot of them, that I would be nowhere without many people, including my parents, but above everybody else, there is Jill, who has saved my life more than once.

I have been going through old emails from July 2010 and

onward, reading the messages I sent her and what she sent back. I cannot believe her patience, and I cannot believe just how bad it got for me. But she never gave up on me. In late September, I alluded to how I didn't think I could go on much longer if this was the way I was going to feel. She wouldn't have it. The messages were long both ways and private, but I will share one excerpt that shows her strength, understanding, and encouragement. All in the middle of keeping the family together, while I was essentially absent.

She wrote: "Tonight we are going to go for a family walk because you can do it and because you should. Tomorrow I want you to go for a short bike ride around the neighbourhood. I'm not taking no for an answer."

I don't know if I did these things or not. I must admit, knowing myself and where I was, I probably found a way out of it. What I do know is that she never would have stopped trying, just like she never would have given up on me, even if I had given up on myself. Everybody needs somebody like that. One of the vital things you need when you're going through mental health challenges is somebody who can be your Jill. Find it in one-on-one therapy, in group therapy, within your social circle, in your family, or in your spouse or partner. You cannot do it alone, and no matter how much you might feel or believe it, you are not alone. If you're reading this and you are not somebody who is working through mental health challenges, be the person that somebody needs, if you can do so. Hopefully, reading this story encourages you to understand somebody else's story, their struggles, and ways you can help.

It was my "get busy living or get busy dying" moment. I was in bed, as usual, in the evening, after work, after supper, waiting for the day to end, and hoping, somewhere in the back of my mind, that tomorrow I'd wake up and be well. Of course, it doesn't work that way. It doesn't work without doing the work. Jill came into the bedroom, sat beside me on the bed, and told me (she didn't ask me) that I needed to go out and get groceries. She had too much to do; we needed food, and it was the only option.

"I can't do it," I said.

I had a vision of walking inside the grocery store, making it down maybe one aisle, and then crumpling to the ground, leaving a nearly empty cart unattended. Somebody would call 9-1-1, and I'd take my third ambulance ride in six months. Maybe I would survive, maybe I wouldn't. I didn't think that I would. It seemed to take everything out of me walking around the house for a few minutes, so I wasn't sure how Jill expected I would make it through an entire trip to the grocery store. And it wasn't only the significant amount of walking that was required in what I knew was a large building; it was pushing a cart that would become gradually heavier the farther I went, filling the car up with bags of groceries, and, worst of all, unloading the groceries and carrying heavy bags from the car into the house, trip after trip after trip. The only time I'd stayed on my feet for any significant length of time was at my book launch, which had taken a lot out of me. I'd made it through, but just barely. A trip to the grocery store and everything it required was asking too much of me, and I couldn't believe Jill didn't see that.

"I'll die," I added, and I would say I added the words dramatically, only I didn't think I was being dramatic; I truly believed that I would die.

"What do you think is wrong with you?" Jill asked.

I understood the confusion. I'd not complained of only one symptom over the months of my breakdown. It had been one thing and then another, sometimes multiple symptoms at once. Heart palpitations, headaches, twitching muscles, weakness, trembling, numbness, tingling, bloating, diarrhea, stomach pains, insomnia, visual disturbances, depression, suicidal ideation, and much more. If you had lived with me for every moment of it, had listened to me complain or freak out about all those things, you would also have asked what was wrong with me. You would have had no clue what was wrong with me. And I had no idea what to say, either. All I knew was that I was not getting better; I was getting incrementally worse, and there was no end in sight, no hope that I would get well.

"Do you really think you're dying?" she asked when I'd not offered a response.

"Yes," I finally said.

I was lying in bed with the lights off. I would be lying in bed for the foreseeable future until I would, at some point soon, trade a bed for a coffin.

"If you really think that you're dying," she said, in a careful, measured tone, "is this how you want to spend the rest of your life?"

I had nothing to say. I feared dying. I had always feared dying. That fear had compounded into a concern for every little thing, a concern that the symptoms in my body, symptoms that I had caused through a massive amount of untreated anxiety, would deliver me to what I was most afraid of.

The sum of my fear.

But if I was certain that death was imminent, and there was nothing I could do to avoid it, why allow it to have that sort of hold over me?

There was no magic button that would cure my anxiety or make me feel well overnight, no matter how much I hoped for that to happen or prayed in my most desperate moments. I used to stay up at night in the dark talking to either nobody or God, crying as I begged for release from what I was going through. I couldn't outrun the fear, but I could stop running and, instead, walk with it.

Or, in this case, go shopping with it.

I took it one step at a time. I got out of bed. I took off my pyjama bottoms and got dressed. Jill gave me the grocery list, and I took it with me out the door. And I think it was important that she didn't make a big deal out of me going, whether she thought it was or not. She acted as though everything was normal, everything was fine, and it was just a regular thing that I was going out to shop. Because it ought to have been. I got in the car and drove to Superstore on Sargent Avenue. I put a loonie in a cart and took the cart with me inside the building. I placed the grocery list on the toddler's seat like I used to do when grocery shopping was a regular occurrence, so that I could check off items as I went along. Then, product by product—a box of spaghetti, a carton of eggs, a jug of orange juice, a loaf of bread—I meandered through the aisles, pushing a cart that, as I'd feared before coming, grew heavier by the second.

But an odd thing happened as I worked my way down Jill's list, which was not insignificant (after all, we had four children). We spent more on groceries than anything else, even our mortgage. I felt a little better with each product I placed into the cart. I felt a little stronger. My knees didn't feel like they might buckle with each step I took. I felt more like myself than I'd felt since July. By the time I'd checked off every item on the list, I knew I could do it again if I had to. The weight that had been crushing me wasn't gone, but it was lighter, and I walked out of the store with hope. I wasn't a lost cause. Who knew? Going to get groceries instead of staying in bed may have been the catalyst for my journey out of that deep, dark hole.

SIX
NOT ALONE

Grocery shopping may have been the catalyst, but it was only the first step of many. I was standing at the bottom of a long flight of stairs, and, as I've told you, I hate stairs. If most people's greatest fear is public speaking, one of my greatest is a staircase. I tried to focus not on the top of the stairs but on the next step up. You cannot get where you need to go without taking it one stair at a time.

It's kind of like learning how to walk.

One of the greatest joys of parenting is watching your baby take steps for the first time, but it doesn't happen easily. There's a progression. They hold their head up, building the strength in their neck. Next, they sit, first with help, something wrapped around them to keep them from falling, and then finally without help. They stand. They pull themselves onto their feet and steady themselves by clutching the edge of the couch. They stand on their own, their arms out to maintain balance. They take their first step. But just one before they fall. Eventually, they take two steps, then three, and soon enough, they're walking. It's empowering, liberating, and it opens a whole world of possibilities.

Overcoming those first six months of crippling anxiety following my nervous breakdown required the same sort of progression, where one step allowed for another, and that next step allowed for another still. Surviving my trip to the grocery store led to me pushing a heavy cart across the parking lot to my car, which led to loading the grocery bags into the trunk, which led to me driving home and unloading those grocery bags, and then I helped Jill put the groceries away.

I like to think that I slept better that night, that I woke up around one or two in the morning, turned around, closed my eyes, and fell back asleep. I like to think that when Jill next told me I was going for a walk around the block with the family, I went; that when she told me to bike around the neighbourhood, that she wouldn't take no for an answer, I got on my bike and toured the neighbourhood, slowly but steadily. Some of this might have happened, some may not have, but going to the store was the first time I did what my little monsters told me I could *not* do. My anxiety was whispering into my ear the things that could happen to me if I went to get groceries, whispering that I would be safer if I stayed home in bed, and while I heard my anxiety loud and clear, I ignored it, and I found that next time, the monsters were quieter than they had been before.

Immediately following my nervous breakdown, my doctor referred me to a psychiatrist. He must have known me better than I knew myself at the time, at least from a medical perspective, because the psychiatrist specialized in health anxiety. Hypochondriasis. I get it. My doctor had been with me since I turned eighteen and had, with patience, fielded all my questions through all my visits and dutifully performed tests, if only to give me comfort—comfort that I could never accept—that what I was worried about, whatever it was, was not what was wrong. He may have been wrong about my heart issue, in my opinion, but I can say with confidence that he was not wrong to make that referral. It wouldn't be until the new year, when I was slowly beginning to put myself back together, piece by piece, that I'd finally get an appointment with her. By then, I'd been waiting almost nine months, which is the give and take of the Canadian health-care system. I looked forward to my first appointment, though. I was not so brazen to think that I didn't need any further interventions, since I'd managed to get some groceries. I knew I had a long road ahead of me, and I knew, as well, that I needed a guide who was more than support. I was feeling better, but I was not well. Being myself again was a long way off. I was still exhausted often, physically, mentally, and emotionally. Tired from not getting enough sleep, tired of dealing with the never-ending parade of symptoms that had not gone away, only had become more manageable. Because I knew now, in the back of my mind, though often I didn't acknowledge it, that I was not dying, that everything was likely the result of anxiety. But in the front of my mind? There was a phrase that I'd uttered too many times to count.

Can anxiety do this?

The mind is a powerful thing. It can do incredible things. It can do incredibly awful things.

The first session I had with my psychiatrist, I spent most of the hour crying. I saw her about once per week to start, and with each session, I cried less, and we started working towards goals; for example, I was not going to google any symptoms over the next seven days. It was unbelievably hard not to give in to the compulsion that I'd made a habit out of, something I did almost without thought, like breathing. If I felt short of breath, I was not allowed to search for potential causes for my shortness of breath on the internet. Why? The internet lacks context. You can google "why do I feel short of breath," and Google will spit out a thousand reasons, most of them terrifying. You would never include in your desperate search that you live with anxiety, nor is there any mechanism to do so. If you acknowledge that you have anxiety and you google "potential symptoms of anxiety," one of the things you will find is "shortness of breath."

When you are disaster googling, you're inviting fear into your life. It's almost like, in some messed-up way, you want the fear, because after you live so long with anxiety, it's a part of you. What would you be without it? You don't want to know that anxiety causes shortness of breath; you want to see the number-one response for a "shortness of breath" search, which is carbon monoxide poisoning. You switch your search from "shortness of breath" to "symptoms of carbon monoxide poisoning," and down the rabbit hole you go. Before you know it, you are in the car, going to Canadian Tire, where you buy carbon monoxide detectors. When the results are negative for the presence of carbon monoxide in your house, you move down to the second item on the list. Heart attack. Well, shit. What are the other symptoms of a heart attack? You google that too.

But what if you searched for "physical symptoms of anxiety"?

- dizziness
- tiredness
- fast, irregular heartbeat
- muscle aches and tension
- trembling or shaking
- **shortness of breath**
- sweating
- stomach ache
- headache
- pins and needles
- insomnia
- and a whole bunch of other stuff

Googling symptoms for anxiety becomes a habit, and it's a habit that needs to be broken. I still scan my body almost all day, and it's mentally exhausting. There are times when I'm distracted and granted relief from the constant scanning, but for the most part, I'm *always* searching for something that isn't quite right. After years of work and refusing to give in to the need to research symptoms on the internet, I never do it. Ever. And I'm better for it. I have my psychiatrist to thank for that, for one of the goals we set together. Another goal was to go for walks, short ones at first. Something achievable so that I didn't fail, so I felt a sense of accomplishment when I made it to the end of the block and back. Next, I would walk to the end of the block and then a few houses farther before turning around and coming home. Eventually, I would walk two blocks, then three. Every week brought with it more goals, some that directly addressed destructive behaviours I'd developed, some that got me off the couch and onto my feet, and some that were more concerned with making me go out and do fun things again. Go out with the kids to the park. Watch a movie at the theatre with my brother-in-law. All of this helped, even if in the smallest amounts.

I also came to accept that effective therapy, for some people, involves more than cognitive behavioural therapy (CBT), which was what I was doing with a kind of exposure therapy when I went for my walks. With the severe anxiety I had, I needed a bit more support in addition to the CBT so that I could function. Despite the work I was doing, despite the steps I had taken, I still wasn't doing as much as I should have at my job; I was still spending too much time in bed; I was still waking up early in the morning and not able to fall back asleep, and it was getting in the way of my progress.

My nerves were in a constant state of fight-or-flight. My anxiety is very physical. It manifests itself with mental symptoms, of course, but even more so with physical symptoms that are hard to deal with. I needed a break from all this anxiety, and I was not going to heal on my own because it is a vicious circle—symptoms lead to worry, worry leads to symptoms. When I started therapy, I had been too worried to take medication that was designed to alleviate the effect worry had on my brain and, in turn, my body. The tiny blue pill my father had placed on my tongue had been an anomaly; if it had eased my anxiety at all, I refused to admit it; I refused to see it.

I had a prescription for anti-anxiety medication, alprazolam, that I had filled, but at the time I started seeing my psychiatrist, I'd not taken any. I would sit on the edge of my bed holding the bottle in my shaking hand, the lid open, staring at those little white tablets, and I could not make myself put one into my mouth. But after several appointments with my psychiatrist, I accepted that medication was a necessary part of my recovery, so one night, sitting on my bed, holding the bottle in my shaking hand, the lid open, I dropped a pill onto my palm and swallowed it with a glass of water. The impact on my body was almost immediate, and it gave me relief that I'd not felt since my breakdown. I could not believe that I hadn't taken medication before, aside from the lorazepam Dad had placed onto my tongue; I wondered how many months I'd made myself suffer more than I had to be suffering. But I tried to move forward thinking of Dad and his advice about regret. Taking meds has helped me, though it's something that changes depending on what's going on in my life. Over the fifteen years since my nervous breakdown, I've had months where I've taken anti-anxiety medication regularly—8:00 a.m. and 2:00 p.m. every day—months where I've taken them as needed on hard days or during panic attacks, and months where I've not needed them at all.

The difficult thing for me was choosing the right support, because it's far too easy to confuse a crutch and support. There are subtle differences between the two, and it's easy to convince yourself that a crutch is a support because it enables you to do things you feel like you couldn't do otherwise. Making the right decisions on what to use comes with experience. Like anything else in life, it's a journey, and making mistakes is a part of the growth process. Over time, you make fewer mistakes, and you have more victories.

A support is something that helps you navigate through mental health challenges in healthy, effective ways. There is not one support that works perfectly for everybody. I've read that EMDR and tapping have been effective for a lot of people, but they did not work for me. Of course, there is a possibility that I wasn't committed enough to those practices because I was skeptical, and that contributed to their ineffectiveness in my anxiety journey, but I still believe that different people require different interventions. A trained professional can help somebody figure out what does and does not work for them; it will likely include trial and error.

Exposure therapy, cognitive behavioural therapy, talk therapy, and medication have all been effective supports for me. Sharing what I've been through and what I'm afraid of and then facing those fears by ignoring the voice that tells me to be afraid have all been a boon to my mental health. There's a strategy I've incorporated into my life lately that I didn't have in 2010/11, and that has been effective in its infancy. I saw it on TikTok, one of several social media apps I've used to follow other people's journeys, along with Instagram and Reddit, where there are some excellent forums for those living with anxiety and depression. Sometimes, reading what people are saying helps you understand more about what's going on in your life, because representation matters. In the TikTok clip, Mel Robbins explains that anxiety, in all of its forms, is worrying about something that *has not happened* yet. Anxiety is catastrophizing.

*

Before I tell you about the TikTok strategy, let me first share a personal experience with worrying about things that haven't yet happened.

In the early 2010s, while vacuuming a van we'd purchased from a friend, I noticed droppings that looked like mouse poop. I looked up to see a deer mouse. It scurried off, and I didn't think much of it. On the way home from St. Laurent, a forty-five-minute drive from Winnipeg, I noticed a mouse run by my feet and another mouse, moments later, on the passenger-side floor mat. When I got home, I parked the van and put my cat in the vehicle for a little while. When I checked the van an hour later, I found a dead mouse on the floor. Charlie got a treat, and I thought that was the end of it.

On the way to work the next morning, however, another mouse darted across the dashboard. I stopped by Home Depot on the way to the office to pick up mouse traps. At lunch, I checked on the traps, and every single one of them had caught a mouse. There were almost ten dead mice throughout the van. As the saying goes, if you see one mouse, there are hundreds of mice; I couldn't imagine how many mice were living in that van.

It started innocently when I searched the internet for ways to get rid of mice from my car. One of the results from that search mentioned hantavirus. The next thing I knew, throughout the course of one afternoon, I was an expert on hantavirus. I knew the symptoms, knew the rate of survival (about 70 percent), and knew how many people had contracted it in Manitoba over the last several decades. Within a few hours, I'd gone from finding dead mice in my car to being 100 percent positive that I had been exposed to hantavirus. The incubation period of hantavirus is, at most, six weeks. I started a countdown from that day to six weeks in the future.

Before the mouse incident, I'd been seeing my psychiatrist less. I'd been doing well. We'd worked through many things, and I was reaching most of our goals. The mice put me back into therapy. I'd stopped obsessively checking my body for symptoms, but now I started to do it more than ever before. One of the early symptoms of hantavirus is an elevated temperature, so I used to go everywhere with a thermometer. When Jill took it away, which she was right to do, I bought another and hid it so she couldn't find it. I checked my temperature more than fifty times a day. Each time, it was normal, but that gave me no comfort. It meant that the incubation period was not over yet. Sooner rather than later, I would get the virus, and I would die from the virus. I wrote goodbye notes to my children. I planned what I would do if I developed more serious symptoms, because early intervention was the difference between death and survival. The chances of contracting hantavirus when exposed to deer mice are something like 1 percent. One percent was somehow more likely than the 99 percent chance I was fine. All of this was textbook anxiety.

The least likely outcome becomes the most likely scenario.

The solution I found on social media is simple; the practice required to get there is difficult (but please use caution when incorporating practices discovered on platforms like TikTok; it might be a good idea to run it by a professional first, especially if it involves something more than simply counting and reciting an affirmation). When you envision the worst possible outcome of something, recognize what you're doing and then start a countdown: 5, 4, 3, 2, 1. When the countdown is over, replace the certainty of the worst possible outcome with a question:

"What if it all works out?"

The idea is to interrupt the disaster thinking by inserting another thought.

"What if I die from hantavirus?" thus becomes "What if everything is going to be fine?"

Mel Robbins, whom I mentioned before, says, "You can't argue with that. If you can stabilize your thoughts, your body settles down, and it doesn't escalate." The question you ask yourself doesn't have to be "What if it all works out?" Robbins says you can use another question or even a statement of affirmation such as "I can do this," but you must interrupt those negative thoughts and replace them with something else.

Medication has been a support and a crutch. It's an easy solution, isn't it, when you have a little white pill (or pink, depending on the dosage) that can sever the impact your mind has on your nervous system and body? It's a pharmaceutical pathway to calm and relaxation. There's a time for it. When my anxiety was so bad that I couldn't think straight or eat, when it had gotten so out of hand that I needed a way to move forward, alprazolam helped me achieve functionality. There's a picture of me, in either December 2010 or 2011, where I look rail thin. I'm wearing a shirt that used to fit me snugly, but it's now hanging off my body. At my heaviest, when I was not taking great care of myself pre-2010, I hovered around 227 pounds. Though I can't recall the exact year, I do know, because it was such a striking change, that I dropped to 187 pounds. I was forty pounds lighter. *Forty pounds.* How much is forty pounds? Four gallons of paint. The average human leg. Five small dogs. An elephant's heart. I wasn't 227 at the time of my breakdown, but I wasn't far off from it, so I lost an enormous amount of weight quickly, and that's more than unhealthy; it's dangerous.

This was around the time when I thought I had stomach cancer and convinced my doctor to refer me to a specialist, who gave me an endoscopy that I had with no sedation. You have to give yourself leeway to get through a panic attack or a bad day with non-medical solutions. You can't instantly reach for alprazolam. You can do things to get yourself through a moment of panic. Deep breathing is something I've done, and I've had many characters in my books do it as an example to others. Breathe in through your nose for five or six seconds, hold it, then breathe out through your mouth for seven or eight seconds, ensuring that every breath you draw in goes straight into your belly. It's a highly effective and proven technique to calm your system. If you try that and it's still not working, maybe it's time to have that pill. There have been times when alprazolam has been the automatic solution, when I have reached for that orange pill bottle before trying anything else. I've taken measures to pull myself out of that habit when I've recognized it. I have travelled a great deal since I started writing, from one end of the city to another, or to

Calgary, Vancouver, Hong Kong, or Hawaii. I have become a more efficient and reliable packer, although I occasionally forget to bring something. Mostly sweaters. But I never *forget* my medication. These days, I have three bottles that I take in my backpack: my beta blockers, my antidepressants, and my alprazolam. I used to only have alprazolam. On some trips, because I knew that I'd fallen into the habit of taking it rather than utilizing strategies I'd learned from my psychiatrist, I would deliberately leave it behind. This would force me to deep breathe, for example, rather than swallow a pill. I worked to move medication from being a crutch back to a support.

The thing is, I've used crutches for a long time. I've used them for different things as I moved from youth into adulthood. Alcohol is a crutch for a lot of people, and it has been for me. When I was young, I drank for the same reasons as a lot of kids. Showing up to a bush party with a two-four is cool, especially when you're underage. For most of my life, I've been insecure. It's not something I've shared often, but it's true. It's due to a bunch of factors. One is my disconnect from my identity and not feeling people would like me if they knew me. I didn't like myself when I was younger, and it's taken years of work to develop a strong sense of self and pride in who I am as an Indigenous person, but alcohol never helped me get there. What it did was make me more outgoing to overcome my shyness. Drunk Dave was fun Dave. I didn't think I was all that fun without a beer or two. Another thing about me is that I tend to wallow in sadness or self-pity.

Rather than try to escape it, I fall into it. One night in the early 2000s, a few years after my grandfather died in 1998, I was writing while Jill was out. I was using Grandpa's electric typewriter, which was the device I wrote poetry and stories with for many years. Writing on a typewriter is the best feeling in the world, to a writer, anyway. That night, I was working on a poem about my grandfather. I still have it today.

His Thoughts (for Mickey)

His thoughts could dwell behind the brow
His thoughts, these words could never stress
Written with a challenged pen
Adept, though not quite air from chests

What thing could lock them safe away?
These bursts of early morning hope
Courageous, halting mindless winds
If fate would but allow them spoke

They might linger with the evening sky
Painted gold from Midas' hands
And dance with such a dizzy joy
With harmony like marching bands

They might tickle the most eager minds
With wisdom smooth as rivers run

Taking fears that chill the soul
Then setting them just as the sun

They might captivate like falling rain
Warm us with a rainbow smile
Remind us of the easy love
That softens falls like leaves in piles

They might have carried us like friendly waves
Deepened us like ocean skies
Prayed with us to keep you safe
Or readied us to say goodbye.

My grandfather's name was Maxwell Eyers, and people called him Mickey. While I worked on the poem, I had a bottle of hard liquor on the coffee table beside the typewriter. The liquid in the bottle rippled from the whir of the machine. I'd watch the tiny, perfect circles when thinking about the next line. At some point, I got so drunk that I stopped writing and began sobbing. When Jill got home, she found me on the floor, crying, the typewriter still on, the bottle almost empty. That's a crutch. Back then, I was not trying to get rid of the pain; I was inviting it in. Things changed after my nervous breakdown. My mind and body were in such a state of constant chaos, a never-ending storm I couldn't escape, and when my anxiety was bad, I'd do anything to get rid of it. Initially, as I've explained, anti-anxiety medication was not something I trusted, but alcohol and I were old friends, and when

I had a drink or two, my anxiety didn't feel as bad. I say I didn't feel as bad, but it *was* as bad. I was placing a bandage over a gaping wound. But that hour or two of relief? I'd take it. I took it, but it was an unhealthy way to deal with what I was going through. I knew that then, and I know that now. But it's so easy. It's too easy.

Still, I don't think I fall into the comfortable stereotype of the drunken Indian, but you have to understand why there are Indigenous people who are struggling with substance abuse issues. There is unresolved trauma in Indigenous communities, families, and individuals from the impacts of colonialism, including the Indian residential school system; the Sixties Scoop; the epidemic of missing and murdered Indigenous women, girls, and Two-Spirit people; and more. There is insufficient support for people who have experienced trauma, and without the tools to address that pain in healthy ways, alcohol, for example, is an accessible numbing agent. Of course, there are other historical factors that have made alcohol a long-term problem, like its provision to Indigenous people during the fur trade, but that's for another conversation. All I want is for people to understand, maybe do a bit of research, and certainly practise empathy and kindness. I digress.

The crutch for me, primarily, has been alcohol. And so, a few years ago, I decided to cut it out of my life entirely. It wasn't good for my anxiety, my depression, my mental health challenges, and it wasn't good for my heart. It wasn't good for anything. I've not had a drink since I turned forty-one. It's been a good change, and the question I asked myself when I decided to quit was: How do I want to live with my challenges? How do I want to address them? Do I want to use a support that works, that might require more effort, but will benefit me in the long term? Or do I want to use a crutch that is easy, that will benefit me for a couple of hours, after which I'll wake up with a headache, and it'll ruin my day? And it will make my anxiety worse, not better. It's not an easy choice, but it's an obvious one.

My psychiatrist enrolled me in group therapy, which was not something I was keen on. Anxiety is an odd paradox. There can be shame associated with it. You feel weak if you're going through it, especially if it's new. When people ask why you've changed, or your kids wonder why you didn't join them for supper or the hike at Birds Hill Provincial Park, or your employer questions why you've been missing so many days, you aren't sure what to say. You might lie about it. Other people can deal with stress in their lives, with worry, and it doesn't blow up in the same way it blew up in your life, so what's wrong with you? The result is that you push yourself away from people right when you need them most because of the embarrassment, because of that feeling of weakness. You need people, but you feel so isolated and detached from everybody, and even when you're there, you're not really there. Anxiety, depression, and all the baggage they bring create the loneliest feeling. You need support to carry the weight, the weight that's crushing you, but you won't ask for it. You tell yourself that nobody can understand what you're going through. You think you're the only person in the world who feels the way you do. How could anybody feel as awful as you feel? How could anybody help?

Then you meet somebody who understands. You meet some-body who has gone through, or is going through, what you are. The things that they're saying about their experience with mental health, even if the subject of their worry is different from yours, are things you can see in your own experience. There is a connective tissue, and that makes you feel less alone. It makes you realize that you are *not* alone. When you know that you're not alone, when you know that other people are going through what you're going through, that knowledge becomes perhaps the greatest support of all. Not only are their struggles your strug-gles, but their victories can be your victories.

I started group therapy skeptically, though. I didn't want to talk about my anxiety; I couldn't see the value in it. But I went, mostly because I was desperate for anything that would help. To that point, some things had, and some things had not. The ses-sions were held in the psychiatrist's office—everybody there was also a patient of hers. I got there early. I usually arrive early to appointments, just like Dad. I hate being late. One by one, people trickled in, and it seemed to me that they were throwing out the same vibe I was. Their skepticism mirrored my skepticism.

It was quiet. Subdued. Our psychiatrist introduced group therapy, and then we went around the room and introduced our-selves. What I noticed most is that there were people from all walks of life—all different ages, genders, styles, and everything else. That could have been a polarizing reality, but we quickly found out, as we introduced ourselves and our struggles, that al-though we were all very different, we shared one important thing.

Anxiety.

In this case, health anxiety.

And this is not to say that everybody there had the same concerns that I had. I'm not sure how they could. At that point in time, I'm not sure I knew what my concerns were. They seemed to change all the time. Some days, it was my heart. On other days, it was the pressure on my head. On still other days, it was twitching in a muscle. I was worried about anything and everything. My anxiety doesn't discriminate. The unifying factor, something that I had discovered in my private sessions, was that the worry about this symptom or that symptom was a fear of death. That whatever was wrong with me would lead to my death, the same thing I now realize I was afraid of when I was a child. If I knew that something I was feeling wasn't going to lead to my death, I wasn't afraid of it, and so there was no anxiety associated with it. It's hard to get to that point, though. Your worry is irrational, it's unreasonable, so you get to the worst possible outcome pretty damn fast.

I'm in Michigan right now. My son's here for the main camp of a team he's been tendered by in the United States. I've got a cold. *A cold.* It's not a mild cold, but it's a cold. At least, I think it's a cold. But what if it's not? What if it's something else that's causing my cough, my runny nose, my sneezing, the sore chest, the headache, the detached feeling? What if I have COVID for the third time, and it's the bad kind? What if I suddenly get super sick, and there's nothing I can do because I've waited too long to do anything about it? It spirals from there. The worst possible outcome is by far the least possible outcome. The most likely outcome is I'm sick, I'll get better, and maybe I should go and get some cold medication while I'm here. I'm nervous about how different the cold medication is in the States, if it'll cause symptoms that make things worse, but I'll try to get through that.

5. 4. 3. 2. 1. "What if it all works out? What if it's just a cold?"

I'm fine. Everything's fine.

I may not believe it, but if I tell myself enough, I can insert a different thought into my inner dialogue, one that disrupts the disaster thinking.

Back to the group therapy.

Not everybody had the same worry as I did, but what I found out was that the behaviours, what I call the mechanisms of anxiety, were very familiar. So, if I had a headache, somebody else had stomach issues, somebody else was afraid of heart disease, another thought they had lupus, but the things we did to address those fears, the unhealthy things, the obsessive things, were almost universal. They were shockingly similar. When we talk about representation, we talk about connections to others who share lived experiences. Those connections are empowering and cathartic. Just as I hope that people who read this story connect with something in it that mirrors experiences in their own lives, I can look at the experiences of the people I met in group therapy and see my challenges with mental health mirrored in theirs.

I've talked about the roots of mental health issues, that whatever those issues are, there seems to be a catalyst. My health anxiety stems from a childhood fear of death and the unknowable chasm of infinity. Whatever the catalyst or seed, it grows until it matures and manifests in a certain way. Whichever way that is, it connects to the root. Health anxiety is the identification of a symptom, and then assigning that symptom, and by association yourself, the worst possible outcome. Paying too much attention to the symptom can, ironically and detrimentally, make matters worse. I cannot count how many innocuous, non-life-threatening symptoms I've exacerbated through worry. In group therapy, I discovered, again, that I wasn't the only person who did this. It was a common experience.

While I won't share a specific instance from therapy out of respect for privacy, because there is a common experience, I can provide an example that reflects what I heard from almost every person I met in that small assembly. Let's say you notice bumps in your throat one day while you're flossing your teeth. You stop flossing and pay full attention to the back of your throat. You angle your mouth under the light to get a better view of the bumps; you haven't seen them before, and they're discoloured. When the vanity light isn't enough, you use the flashlight on your cellphone. But the flashlight isn't bright enough, and the white light it emits isn't very accurate, so you go to the garage, find an industrial flashlight, and start to obsessively check your throat multiple times throughout the day. The more you shine light into your throat, the more worried you become. You touch the bumps with your index finger to check their texture. It makes you gag, but you need to know how they feel so you can provide Google with more information. Your spouse recognizes the destructive behaviour, so they take away the flashlight to circumvent the spiral you're about to experience. They tell you to go to a clinic if you're worried, so you do, and they tell you it's nothing to worry about. On the way home from the clinic, you buy another flashlight so you can secretly keep looking at the bumps. You poke at them with one of the wooden skewers in the cutlery drawer because it makes you gag less, and you can reach farther back into your throat. Where does it end? A few years later, when you're not dead from throat cancer, you concede that it was likely nothing and finally let it go. Here's the thing. If you shine a flashlight inside your mouth, down your throat, you'll see a bunch of weird things. And if you poke at it? Prod it? You're going to cause a scratchy sensation or soreness, which becomes a symptom because you're irrational and don't attribute it to the cause but rather to your fear.

For everybody, there was a root, a progression, a manifestation or maturity, and obsessive behaviours, and those behaviours either worsened or created symptoms that spiralled into a cycle that was hard to break. There were different ways in which each person sought to numb the symptoms brought on by their anxiety, and it seemed as though the point where some people were at, or some people were getting to, was depression. When you're stuck in that loop and don't see a way out, you feel like your life is the sum of your struggles.

But I learned something, above anything else, in group therapy. As much as we shared trauma, baggage, unhealthy machinations, the mechanisms of mental health, of anxiety and depression, of obsessive-compulsive behaviours and compulsions, and all the bad things we brought into that room, there was another commonality. If we suffered in the same way, we could survive in the same way. If we hurt in the same way, we could heal in the same way. Look at something like exposure therapy. Whatever you want to call it. I would classify it less elegantly and label it as "telling your anxiety to fuck off."

I won't share a specific example from group therapy, but here is a hypothetical situation that represents what I would call a common experience.

Let's say there was a person in our group concerned with germs who would never touch anything without wearing surgical gloves or sanitizing or washing their hands immediately after contact with whatever they had touched. If they were entering a shopping mall and had put their hand on the door handle to enter the building, before doing anything else, they would take out a miniature bottle of sanitizer, slather their hands, and, once that was done, continue with their expedition. Or they would bring a cloth to cover the handle so they wouldn't have to make direct contact (and subsequently throw out the cloth immediately afterwards). A little monster on their shoulder whispered to them, "If you touch that with your bare hand, or if you touch that and don't disinfect your hand right away, you're going to get sick. You could get sick with something and die." What action would they need to take to begin to overcome that anxiety, the thing whispering in their ear?

We were tasked with figuring that out during the week between sessions. What action could you take to ignore that voice and, by doing so, quiet it? We named a fear and then committed to an action in front of everybody else in the group. That fostered accountability.

In the situation I've fabricated, the person would have to touch a public surface and not immediately clean their hands. Imagine they took a bus to work one morning and hung on to a handle. They wouldn't wash their hands until they got to the office, ignoring any compulsion to use their bottle of sanitizer.

Contrary to their fears, they didn't get sick. Now, their anxiety didn't show itself in a physical way as mine does, but sickness is sickness, and wellness is wellness. They had been sick, they still were sick, but they'd started a healing journey not dissimilar to being afraid to walk or stay on your feet for an extended period of time and yet going grocery shopping.

This didn't happen in my group, but it could have. How do I know that for sure? Because it did, only with real people who had real anxieties.

This is not radical therapy. People do things to overcome their fears daily, and the result is always the same. At the swimming pool, a kid walks to the end of a five-metre platform. They stand at the edge with their toes curled over the side. They look down, and it seems as though they're a mile high. They're frozen with dread and stand there for five minutes with their parents and siblings beside the pool, shouting encouragement. Eventually, they take a deep breath, step forward, and jump. What do they do when they get out of the pool? They run up to the five-metre diving board again, and this time, they don't hesitate. There are no specific, universal acts one can take to overcome anxiety, but there are universal practices that can help. Exposure therapy is one of those practices. That voice does not go away, but you learn to respond, "I *hear* you, but I'm not *listening* to you."

These are all steps on a journey. There might be a cure for anxiety. I've heard people talk about that, that they're cured of anxiety. If that's possible, that's great. This is not my experience so far, and I'm okay with that. If I came to the point where my struggle with mental health was entirely relieved, I'm not sure what that would mean for who I am. It's come to define who I am. It's as much a part of my identity as it is to be Cree or to be a father or a writer or a husband. All of that is the stuff of David, and I would not be who I am without it. It made me weak, and it still does sometimes, or at least it makes me perceive myself as weak, but now I try to look at it as something that helps to make me strong. Because it's not a weakness. Michael Landsberg, a fierce and vital mental health advocate and sports journalist, calls himself a mental health warrior and coined the phrase "Sick Not Weak." I try to make those words louder than the voice in my ear. Anxiety is a mental health illness. So is depression. Although it affects your body, it's an illness of the mind. You don't feel weak and inferior when you have a cold, and nor should you when you have a mental health illness. You don't need cough syrup for it, but you need proper treatment. That can come in the way of therapy, medication, or a combination of both. I have tried many types of therapy, as well as medication, and it can be a trial-and-error thing, until you eventually find what works for you.

By far the most effective treatment for my mental health challenges has been sharing with others. I credit my experience in group therapy for this. If it weren't for the time I spent sitting in a room with strangers, once a week, for several sessions, I would not have come to this realization. By the end of the sessions, we weren't strangers. We had become a community. We built community through stories of truth that we shared with one another, by recognizing our own truths represented in those stories. If the hardest thing about having anxiety is a feeling of isolation, that nobody can understand what you're going through, then what happens when you discover that people *do* understand, that they *have* been through what you've been through, that they *have* fucked up like you've fucked up, that they feel the same hopelessness you feel?

You stop *suffering* from anxiety and begin to *live with* anxiety.

That's a big difference.

And it isn't just seeing your experience mirrored in others. When I made the decision to actively expand my community of people living with mental health illnesses, of people who were mental health warriors, I found that there were people at varying stages of their journey. I want to say that it became like a mentorship framework. At the step I was at in my journey, I felt as though I had something of value to share with people who were at the beginning steps of their journey. I could pass on what I had learned to the others who had not yet been through what I had been through. I didn't realize it, but through lived experience, through therapy, I was building up a store of knowledge and practices that I could offer to others through stories, and they could hopefully find value in what I had to say. Likewise, there were people further along than I was whom I could learn from, and, most important, I could see that even in the darkest moments, which were still to come, there was a way out of the darkness. I walk ahead of some to show them the way, I follow others who can show me the way, and I walk alongside others who are where I'm at. But we are all on the same journey, and we all want the same thing, and it's somewhere we can get together.

That's community.

SEVEN
JUST BREATHE

Due to the impact group therapy had on me, I knew I wanted to write about my experience with mental health, I just didn't know how. Sharing privately in a small group is one thing; sharing publicly about what you're going through is another. If you move along this mental health journey by taking small steps, one after the other, the same approach makes sense for "going public," especially since it's part of the healing process. If I was going to talk about mental health, initially, at least, I found it was necessary to insulate myself in some way. I needed a vehicle, and one that made sense for me.

As a kid, I was all about superheroes. Not only did I have action figures, and all the best kinds—Transformers, He-Man, G.I. Joe, Star Wars, Visionaries, Battle Beasts, M.A.S.K. (I could go on and on)—but my brother Michael and I read comic books. My favourite has always been Spider-Man. We had boxes of comics. We bought more every weekend with our allowance at STYX Comics on Corydon. We used to draw heroes, too. Mike was the real artist; I just tried to keep up with him. Don't get me wrong: the main reason for my superhero obsession back then was that I thought they were cool. I still love Boba Fett today, and yes, it's mostly because of the armour and the attitude. That head nod in *Return of the Jedi*? Deadly. Soundwave and Snake Eyes check the same boxes.

But if I dig below the surface, and not even that deep, I find another reason I love superheroes so much. It was a form of escapism. And that's one of the beautiful things that stories give us. Time off from our lives in another place, another time. Characters in comics and books become friends we can spend time with and get to know, that feel real to us, that we care about, and that we miss when they're gone. The connection between the reader and the character becomes so intimate that we can also become them. *I* was the guy in the cool suit nodding at Princess Leia in her bounty hunter disguise.

But there is a darker, problematic side to this immersion in comics.

There was a G.I. Joe action figure called Spirit, a Native American character whose real name was Charlie Iron-Knife. Everything about him screams, "I'm an Indian!" in the most stereotypical way. He's a reflection of how Indigenous people were represented in the past, especially in the superhero realm. He's got medicine man/shaman vibes. He wears a headband, leather pants, and what look like mukluks. Sort of. He's got this big knife as a primary weapon. His backstory is no better. He comes from a poor family because, you know, Native Americans are poor, and his secondary military specialty is listed as Social Services. There's probably an awareness there of the fact that most kids in "care" are Indigenous.

And there were even more characters in comics that espoused the same problematic, tired stereotypes. But again, as lazy as it is, and ignorant, it's almost familiar and comfortable. Another example I mention a lot in my talks is Black Bison, or John Ravenhair (they never really have names that aren't "native" in some way. You get a lot of Iron-Knife and Ravenhair, but you don't get a lot of Robertson). He's got the headdress, leather pants, shield, spear, and shamanistic powers. He was possessed by an Elder hell-bent on revenge against the white man (he probably called them pale faces) for what they did to his people. (I'm not mad at an awareness that many of our problems stem from the actions of middle-aged white men, historically and in contemporary society, but I've yet to meet an Elder with revenge or hate in their heart.) Playing with figures and reading characters like Spirit and Black Bison had a negative impact on me; the lie of the Savage Indian (one trope out of a few) helped to create a negative sense of self that I'm still trying to fix decades later. It's one of the reasons why I write stories, and one of the reasons why I chose to write comics before any other form of literature. I've written and talked a lot about this, so I won't belabour the point, but I saw the opportunity to improve representation through this form of storytelling. Comics engage with readers of all ages and genders through the relationship between words and images; they help develop reading skills, teaching everything from English language arts to science to history. They have the potential for positive influence when they have accurate Indigenous characters. So, what would happen if I created a superhero story that included multi-level representation, not just in how it depicted Indigenous characters, but in how it depicted somebody going through mental health challenges?

I saw the potential in playing with tropes of the superhero genre. For example, every superhero has a weakness. Even Superman, the most overpowered superhero ever written, has a weakness: kryptonite. In the movie *Unbreakable*, David Dunn's weakness is water. He's never been sick or injured in his life, but he can drown. I thought, *What if I created a Cree character, a teenager, who had incredible powers, but their weakness was anxiety? Panic disorder? Mental health issues?* Here's the part where you get to play around a little bit. What if, throughout the course of a story, he learns that his mental health issues are *not* a weakness? They are a part of who he is and what makes him a hero. Sick, not weak. When he's about to fight a bad guy but is having a panic attack, he does some deep breathing, takes an anti-anxiety pill, and goes to work. Or he learns to use that nervous feeling in his body, that state of fight-or-flight, for energy, because he has accepted that it won't kill him, and, as the saying goes, what doesn't kill you can make you stronger. I felt like it could work.

All I needed was a vehicle. That was tough. At that stage in my writing career, while I'd written several graphic novels, I'd taken cues from history, historical fiction, and contemporary issues. My stories addressed intergenerational trauma and healing; the Indian residential school system; real-life Indigenous heroes in Canadian history; missing and murdered Indigenous women, girls, and Two-Spirit people; and, in a collection of interconnected short stories, life on-reserve, its difficulties and beauties, and what it looks like to try to leave it all behind but take everything with you anyway. All these books varied in scope and topic, but the through-line was representation.

What I had come to understand was that not only was it important to represent Indigenous people and cultures accurately, but also that mental health needed better representation. There was a stigma attached to mental health issues that I felt needed to be undone; it had contributed to people's unwillingness to share their struggles, which, in turn, worsens feelings of isolation and hopelessness. Accurate representation of characters living with mental health issues could make the same impact as it had made on culture, gender, and sexual orientation. What we're really talking about is destigmatization through normalization. It didn't hurt that I still planned on writing a superhero character that was Cree. The superhero genre, while improving, still needs increasingly better Indigenous representation. Why not kill two birds with one stone?

Before I had any books published, I developed a television series concept with my friend Jeff. I wanted to take everything I loved about television shows, and everything I felt hadn't been done well, and make something I would want to see that emulated some shows while avoiding the mistakes of others. Back then, in the late 2000s leading up to 2010, I was heavily into *Lost* (which is still my favourite show of all time, despite its flaws). I loved the concept of having people trapped on an island, unable to escape the perils they faced, and how the world got bigger the longer they stayed there. I also loved the mythology. So, together, Jeff and I came up with a concept called *The Reckoner*. At its heart, the show would be about a middle-aged Cree guy who made a deal with a trickster spirit to save his friends from a fire and, in so doing, was imbued with (non-stereotypical) superpowers. It was important for me that he didn't have any shamanistic abilities, almost as much as it was important that his *perceived* weakness would be anxiety and panic disorder.

The television show was optioned by a production company, and scripts were written for it. During the development process, though, a lot of things changed. That's unavoidable when you have a bunch of people in a room throwing ideas around. Some of the changes were good; some of them I disliked. The gestation of *The Reckoner* is painful and fraught and something I'd rather not get into (although, appropriately, it caused a lot of anxiety and stress), but suffice to say that eventually, the options ran out, and I saw the opportunity to take back my story. So, I did. I reclaimed *The Reckoner* and decided that it would be the vessel to accomplish the goal I'd set, to present a brand-new accurately and appropriately written Native superhero while at the same time representing and normalizing mental health for what I hoped would be a wide readership. Aside from my short story collection, *The Evolution of Alice*, everything I'd done to that point in my writing career had been for children, and I'd learned that many adults read children's literature.

The Reckoner eventually became a graphic novel series—hopefully, one that is ongoing—but back then, I first wanted to write an origin story. The graphic novels were for an established superhero; with what I wanted to do, in digging deep into my main character's mental health struggles and how his "weakness" would turn into an important part of his identity, I needed the room a novel would give me. Not one young adult novel, but a trilogy. The Reckoner series started with *Strangers*, was followed by *Monsters*, and was rounded out with *Ghosts*. The books were narratively and metaphorically about mental health. In *Monsters*, there is a literal monster in the book, but the title refers to the monster of anxiety. At first, I wanted that monster to be scarier than the monster killing people in the fictional community of Wounded Sky First Nation. I wanted the monster of anxiety to be scary until Cole (named after my son, who does *not* have mental health challenges) faces it and learns how to be a hero while living with it. To walk with it rather than fight against it.

One of the many benefits of writing children's literature since 2009 has been working with students and teachers and librarians. *Strangers* and its sequels, like most of my work, were immediately used in classrooms and stocked in libraries. A big part of my writing career is classroom visits. When kids ask the question, "What's your favourite thing about being an author?" I tell them that it's spending time with them. You'd think it would be writing, but books, though I try my best to write good stories, have become a pathway into schools, to meet the people to whom we really ought to be paying most of our attention.

Something that was at once eye-opening and liberating happened when I visited schools to talk about the Reckoner trilogy and about mental health. At almost every single visit, after all the talking was done and after all the questions had been asked and after I'd signed all the books and children's arms and hats and torn pieces of paper, at least one kid would come up to me during a quiet moment, usually when I was packing up my bag and getting ready to go.

"Mr. Robertson?"

"Hey, how's it going?"

"I just wanted to let you know that I'm going through what Cole's going through."

Most of the time, they were shy, and I could relate to that. It's hard talking about something you've not really talked about before. I think what helped the kids feel safe enough to approach me with their anxiety or depression or panic disorder, or whatever else they might have been living with, was that it wasn't only what Cole was going through; it was what *I* was going through. I was easing my way into being open about my experience with mental health. I did not intend to do it that way at first. I'd not written the Reckoner with the idea that I would spill my guts about my nervous breakdown and everything that followed, but looking back, I suppose that I understood if I were truly going to make a difference in advocating for and normalizing mental health issues, I needed to talk about how it was a part of my life.

It was a good thing I did. Talking about everything I had dealt with and what I was still living with (I'd even had a panic attack right before a classroom visit and told the kids about it) gave them permission and a feeling of safety to talk about the stuff they were dealing with. Almost none of them wanted to make a thing out of it, either. They just wanted to tell me. That's it. And who knows what kind of healing journey that started them on. Not because of me, mind you, but because of a story and how the character in that story reflected their experiences.

What I found, as well, is that mental health issues are indiscriminate. Kids (and sometimes teachers and librarians) approached me who were of different gender identities, different cultural backgrounds, and different ages. That's what was most startling to me:

the pervasiveness of mental health illnesses. Kids in *elementary school* talked to me about their anxiety. I wonder if that would have been me if I'd had the same vocabulary when I was younger.

Woven into the Reckoner trilogy and the story outside of the story are the pillars of support that have helped me live with anxiety. The Reckoner and the books that have followed—like its graphic novel sequel tetralogy the Reckoner Rises and my memoir *Black Water* and novel *The Theory of Crows*—are instructional. Yes, I want people to see themselves in these stories, but I want them to experience more than just a feeling of having been seen. I want readers to walk away from my books with an idea of how they can live better with mental health challenges. Cole becomes more than a hero; he becomes an example and even a teacher. Something he does repeatedly throughout the series is take medication, but while he finds support in pharmaceutical interventions, he incorporates strategies that help to calm him when he's having a panic attack. A big one is belly breathing. He breathes in through his nose for five seconds, right into his stomach, and then out through his mouth for seven seconds. It's something my characters do in *The Barren Grounds* (Morgan, and later, Eli), *Black Water* (me), *The Theory of Crows* (Matthew), and even in my picture book *The Song That Called Them Home* (Lauren).

I'm trying my best to drill home the importance and benefits of deep breathing. That's because it works; it lowers the heart rate, reduces stress hormones, balances oxygen and carbon dioxide levels, and triggers a relaxation response because we breathe slower and in a more controlled way when we are calm. The primary symptom of a panic attack, in my experience, for example, is shallow breathing; this exacerbates panic, the antithesis of calm. When I wrote scenes with Cole practising deep breathing, I imagined kids emulating it. There are other strategies in my books too, like exposure therapy and medication, but it's all meant to reach beyond the page and into the real world.

When I wrote *Black Water*, a memoir about my father and me, about his life, about my life, and how our lives intersected to lead us back to his childhood home on the trapline, a story that addressed my mental health challenges, I felt as if I'd been planning and researching the book for a decade. Dad had always been an enormous part of my career, its focus, its goals, and a lasting presence in my public speaking engagements, so it felt right to put it all on the page. Until the unthinkable happened. I was close to having a final draft of *Black Water* when my father passed away suddenly in December 2019. His loss made rewriting the epilogue, recording the audiobook, and supporting the memoir unbelievably difficult. Difficult and, in the case of supporting the book, vitally important, because I talked about my father and our relationship, of course, but I also expanded the scope of my conversations around mental health beyond the classroom and into the public space through guest lectures, events at literary festivals, freelance journalism, and interviews.

I came to learn the value of balance. I'd learned the same thing in writing about traumatic events in history for Indigenous people. In *When We Were Alone*, a grandmother talks to her granddaughter about having her identity taken away through family disconnect, her hair being cut off, having to wear uniforms, and being forbidden to speak her language. Those acts of violence against a child were not shied away from, but they were tempered with stories of reclamation. The grandmother tells her grandchild that she had her hair cut as a youth in an Indian residential school but speaks to her grandchild about how she always wears her hair long now. Even as a child, she practised small acts of defiance to hang on to her identity—for example, braiding sweetgrass into her hair so it would be long again. I do the same thing with mental health because the goal isn't to traumatize; it is to empower. That's why I write and speak about deep breathing whenever I write or speak about anxiety or panic attacks, and that's why whenever I use the analogy of the little monster sitting on my shoulder, whispering into my ear, I talk about how I try my best not to listen to its voice, and to do things it tells me that I can't do. Ever since my excursion to the grocery store, anyway.

I started writing about anxiety in a more personal, less insulated way in 2019. The first article I wrote was for CBC Parents, and it extended the discussion of intergenerational trauma to show how anxiety can be intergenerational as well. I talked about how my mother has anxiety, how I have anxiety, how my wife has anxiety, and how some of our kids have anxiety. The beautiful thing about that is we can go through it together, and sometimes learn from each other. In the article, I explained how living with anxiety has been hard for me, but living with anxiety is even harder for a child who may not fully understand what they're going through or why.

Lauren, my youngest girl, was crying one day, and when I asked her what was wrong, she said, "I just don't know why I have to be this way." The only thing I could think to do was to empathize, because I could. I acknowledged her feelings and told her I often felt the same way. Empathy is important when it comes to mental health. And listen, we'll all have those "why me" days on this journey. It's okay to have those days. We'll also have days of incredible bravery (and yes, brave can be going to buy groceries). In 2018, my family and I drove all the way to Nova Scotia and back. On the way home, we stopped at Niagara Falls. The kids had never been there before, and it's an impressive attraction. As a tourist attraction there are more things to do than stare in awe at the falls, which truly are awe-inspiring. A couple of my kids, including Lauren, were interested in the zipline, and we agreed to let her go, even though Jill and I were nervous about it. Before strapping Lauren into the seat that would take her on a rather long jaunt to the bottom, over water and land that was far below, my wife told our daughter that she didn't have to go if she didn't think she could; it was okay if she was too scared.

Lauren replied, "Mom, I can do hard things."

And then she went down the zipline all by herself.

I can do hard things. I repeat that in my mind these days, like a mantra, each time the voice in my ear tells me I can't do something, even the smallest thing, even the most ridiculous thing, every day.

I can do hard things, and so can you.

This morning, it told me, "You shouldn't eat that granola; yesterday, it made your palpitations worse." It's true that I had eaten granola the day before, and my skipped heartbeats did flare up. But so what? Every doctor I've seen has told me that it's not fatal. Guess what I had for breakfast today?

The vital outcome of the books, the articles, the interviews, and the public speaking was that it gave others permission to share their stories because I had shared mine. I had friends in my life, mostly from the writing community, who had no clue I was living with anxiety, and likewise, I had no clue they were as well. It brought me closer to those friends, and to the public in general, who felt, and still feel, comfortable enough with me to tell me about their mental health struggles in person or online, like through a message on social media. It's like we all formed one big community. There is a lot of talk in publishing about a writer's platform, which is an author's ability to reach their potential audience. I often think of what I am doing with the platform I have. Dad helped me develop a consideration of not what I *can* do but what I *should* do with whatever reach I have. When he died, I inherited a bunch of his notebooks. On the last one he kept, which had copious notes and quotes and thoughts in it, he'd taped a saying by Edward Everett Hale to the inside front cover that I've since translated into Cree syllabics and tattooed onto my wrist (it's both a tribute and practical, because I lose everything).

I am only one, but still I am one. I cannot do everything, but still I can do something and because I cannot do everything, I will not refuse to do the something that I can do.

If you have the capability to create change, then you have the *responsibility* to create change, even if it's just one thing, because nobody can do everything. To me, that quote by Hale is a synonym for the starfish parable. A young girl on a beach littered with thousands of starfish was throwing them back into the ocean, one by one. A bunch of people watched the girl until one said, "What difference does it make doing that? Look at this beach!" The girl looked deterred momentarily before straightening her posture and throwing another starfish back. "I made a difference to that one." The man became inspired to help the girl, and others joined in until all the starfish were safe. It's a story that combines the "I am only one" quote with the concept of how community is built.

The conversations I have with fellow writers and the messages I get from engaged readers all, in varying degrees, speak to the power of Story and the healing that comes from it. The best support, by far, is to share your experience. I often recall the pantry door in the kitchen, throwing my fist through it, and I consider how it's analogous to my nervous breakdown. I kept everything inside for so long, I suffered in silence, and, eventually, it became too much for me. I blew up, and then everything shut down. It left me with a mess within and outside my body that I've been trying to clean up for almost fifteen years. The most effective way to clean a mess is to clean with other people. Trust me. My son won a hockey championship in 2023, and he invited his whole team over to our house after the game (including friends and girlfriends). When the party was over, at two or three in the morning, I started cleaning it all up. A couple of Cole's friends helped, and things got done faster than they would have otherwise. This is not to say that I'm talking about speed, but it is talking about community.

Community builds and introduces itself in different ways.

A few years ago, a friend of mine who also works in the arts was travelling somewhere in Canada and, out of nowhere, called me from the airport. They were waiting for their plane to board when a panic attack reared its ugly head. They couldn't take a deep breath, their chest felt heavy, and they were sweating—all the typical symptoms. I can't remember whether I was their first call, but I was up there, and I knew why. We'd had numerous conversations about anxiety; we both knew that we lived with it, and calling me when they needed support was safe. While on the phone, I listened to them describe what was going on and how afraid they felt, and then, together, we worked through it. Some of it was gaining control of rational thought (that is, it's not a heart attack; nothing life-threatening is happening), and some of it was deep breathing with me. It's easier sometimes when you're guided in the practice; my father used to do the same thing. He'd put his hand on my stomach and make me raise it and lower it with my breath, and after a few minutes, I would be calm. When I wrote *The Theory of Crows*, which is as close as you can come to autofiction without explicitly writing autofiction, that was a big part of how the main character, Matthew, and his father connected. My friend got on the plane that day; they just needed somebody to hold their hand for a second. We all need that every once in a while.

One of the things I love about working as a writer in the literature scene here on Turtle Island is that it is a community, and within that community, there are smaller suburbs, if you will.

Children's authors have their little suburb. Similarly, Indigenous artists have their suburb. Winnipeg has a tremendous Indigenous literary landscape, and I'm confident in saying that we all know and support one another. Then there's another cross-disciplinary cluster, and that's a community of artists who are living with anxiety. We know each other, have shared with each other, and are there for each other if any of us ever need support.

This brings us to autumn 2019 at Wordfest in Calgary. I'd started to get more actively involved in mental health advocacy by agreeing to speak on panels about it or my experience living with it. You know, the whole imposter syndrome thing is real. As a writer, I have it. For the first couple of years of attending writers' festivals, when I started to get asked to participate in them, I mostly kept to myself. There were two reasons for this. Well, there were several reasons, but two stand out for me. I was still going through some awful mental health challenges, and it felt easier and safer to hang out in my hotel room and be alone unless I had to eat or there was an event I was involved in. In my hotel room, I'd work on a book so it wasn't wasted time, or I'd watch movies or lie in bed feeling sorry for myself, filling my head with thoughts of fear and avoidance, which is very much wasting time and destructive. And I didn't think I belonged. I saw the names of other artists at these festivals and thought, *Who the hell am I?* That's a feeling that hasn't entirely gone away, even today. In 2017, I was hanging out in a hospitality suite packed with a who's who of Canadian literature. I turned one way, and there was Lawrence Hill. I turned another way, and there was André Alexis. I'd just read *Fifteen Dogs*, and he was ten feet away from me. But credit goes to Jill, as it so often does. Very early on in my writing career, she encouraged me to socialize. The Kingston WritersFest in Kingston, Ontario, was the first place I managed to step out of my comfort zone and hang out in the hospitality suite. I walked into the room, and one other writer was sitting on a chair, a manuscript on his lap that he was working on. Thomas King, editing *The Inconvenient Indian*. No big deal. I sat on the couch across from him with a plate sparsely decorated with food I wasn't touching and tried not to bother him, to just accomplish the goal Jill had set out for me. It wasn't long until Thomas introduced himself to me, and we talked. I was terrified at first of saying something idiotic in front of one of my idols, but he was generous with his time and very kind.

Since that time, when I realized that it wasn't as scary as I thought it would be, I've made a point of hanging out in the hospitality suite, even when my anxiety is high. I don't think it's improved my imposter syndrome, but I have learned that even some of the most well-known writers in Canada feel the same way. I'm not one to flex, but I walk into a room, and not many writers have two Governor General's Literary Awards under their belt. I still have that voice saying, *You should not be here. You are not good enough. You won those awards because of [illustrator] Julie [Flett], not because of anything you did.*

(Julie also has two Governor General's Literary Awards for the books, by the way.)

My imposter syndrome has extended into mental health advocacy, and the reasons for this are likely connected; they derive from the same source—anxiety—but there's a bit more to it than that. The voice in my head tells me that I'm not good enough to be in a room with writers I love and admire, even though I bring bona fides with me now that I can objectively acknowledge. I don't need those bona fides, mind you; they just make it easier for me to trick my brain into believing that I belong in a room with other artists. With mental health advocacy, it's not so easy, and I have imposter syndrome relating to my involvement. Is living with anxiety enough to become some kind of voice in speaking about it? To provide peer advice to others going through it? Maybe. Maybe not. That autumn in 2019, walking to the event with my friends while in the middle of a panic attack, it was going through my head that I shouldn't be there, that I didn't have anything to offer, that I'd been living with anxiety for years, and sure, I'd learned strategies, but sometimes it felt as though I was no better off than I was at the start of it all, during my nervous breakdown. If that was true, how could I say anything that would help somebody else? That's not exclusively what started the panic attack that day, but it was a contributing factor.

While I have imposter syndrome with my mental health advocacy, just like I have it with my writing career, that's on me, not on anybody else. With mental health advocacy, I can't shake the thought that I'm a fraud. Not that I don't live with mental health issues, because I totally do. I have generalized anxiety disorder, I have health anxiety, I have obsessive-compulsive disorder, I have depression. I've got all of that, and I always will. How I feel fraudulent is that I talk about mental health, I write about mental health, I present on mental health, I offer support for others who have mental health challenges, I give advice on how to live more effectively with mental health while, at the same time, I screw up almost every single day and give in to those little monsters sitting on my shoulders. I don't do things that I know I ought to do. I have days where I feel no better than I did at the start of my acute experience with anxiety in 2010. I have days where I feel even worse. Much worse. I can give advice, but I often don't take my own advice, and while that's human, it makes me feel like I've failed repeatedly.

My anxiety journey is an ocean of waves of differing sizes. Some waves are small enough that I can push through them. Some are so big that they try to pull me out to sea when they crash over me. They try to drown me. In 2016, my family went on a camping trip all the way to Haida Gwaii. We stopped in Ucluelet, at a camping ground on the western shore of Vancouver Island. We stayed on the beach, about thirty feet from the water. One afternoon, Anna was playing in the water, and a wave came and crashed over her little body. Luckily, I was nearby, and before she was pulled away from the shore, I got a hold of her hand. If I hadn't been there, she might've died. That's what those bad days feel like, and I'm lucky that somebody's been there to hold my hand and keep me from being pulled away. Usually, that person is Jill. Sometimes, it's writer friends or my mother. It used to be Dad. But why do those waves still come, and what does that mean? What does it say about where I'm at and where I'm going? If I keep hanging on by a thread and pushing through, do I have any business doing what I'm doing? Is the journey enough, or, at some point, am I going to have to reach my destination? Or maybe there isn't one. Maybe there's only the journey. The good and the bad.

EIGHT
RELAPSE

I have never known what to expect from one week to another, and for a long time, that was the most frustrating thing about living with mental health conditions: the uncertainty of it. I could go a week or more feeling relatively good. I'd feel good enough that a thought would sneak into my mind that I was through the worst of it. I had no illusions that life would be smooth sailing from that point on, but I held out hope that anxiety would become less and less of a presence in my life and I'd be able to find normalcy. Or, even though I don't love the saying, find contentment with a *new normal*. I wouldn't feel the way I used to when I was young, before my breakdown, but I would feel well enough.

It was headed that way. Within a year or two of having my nervous breakdown, I was back to doing things that I would never have thought possible in 2010. And often, I was doing things not *because* I felt all the way better but *despite* not feeling all the way better. One thing I have not mentioned too much to this point is the importance of exercise for mental wellness. I haven't mentioned it because, for reasons I'm getting to, exercise scares me more than most things. Exercise in all its forms. There was a time when I was on a good track. I used to exercise because

I was having a bad day; I didn't use a bad day as an excuse to avoid exercise.

In the early 2010s, I took to jogging a little bit. From our house on Banning Street, I'd run to Garbage Hill, maybe not go up Garbage Hill in a Rocky-type moment, but around it, and then back to the house. It was a healthy five-kilometre jog. One night, late, I was at the end of an awful day and wanted to go to bed, which had remained my safe place. Instead, I changed into shorts and a tank top, stuck in some earbuds, and went for a short run. I felt better when I was done. Today, that sort of mindset is foreign to me. I'd like to get back to that place. I'm working on building up the courage, and I know that I can do it. After I stopped jogging for a year or so, I picked it back up again (everything about anxiety seems to include ebbs and flows, undulations like ocean waves that you can push through or be pulled out to sea with), but I was in awful shape. I downloaded a "couch to 5k" app on my phone, and after a few months, I was running the distance easily and doing so at a good pace. Around that time, on Father's Day, I finished the race in thirty minutes with a kid on my shoulders (way better than anxiety on your shoulders) and pushing another kid in a stroller. I felt like Super Dad.

I wasn't only jogging. I started playing hockey on Sunday nights, something I'd not done since I was a teenager. I was nervous before the first game I played, not because there was anything riding on it, mind you. It wasn't even beer league. It was just pickup hockey, no refs, no penalties, and mostly all nice guys. My buddy Dan had invited me out, and though I was by far the worst player on the ice, everybody was patient and welcoming, and only some of the better players decided to pick on the ankle-bender. My nervousness originated from a worry that I was about to participate in a far more intense hour of exercise than jogging, where admittedly, though I could run quickly if I wanted to, I often found my own leisurely pace, just enough to break a sweat.

I didn't see the warning signs, or maybe I refused to see them.

I got used to the route I took from home to the rink. I was still living on Banning Street. I'd drive up Arlington Street to Portage Avenue, then turn onto Broadway and follow it to the end, to Main Street. I'd turn right on Main Street, then left on Marion, and tucked in behind an A&W was the Marion Beer Store. Every Sunday, I would stop there on the way to hockey. I'd pick up a beer or two to drink after the game with the guys, which was customary. It's a rite of passage to drink beer after late-night hockey. I'm not so sure the same can be said about drinking beer before hockey, but that's the real reason why I bought alcohol. I justified getting beer by convincing myself it was for after the game, but either in the parking lot at the beer vendor or in the parking lot at Maginot Arena, I would drink a strong beer before going into the rink. I thought that giving myself a buzz and taking the edge off would make things easier, and it did at first. But it was a crutch, and I became reliant on a pre-game beer rather than waiting to enjoy a post-game beer. The positive thing was that I was exercising. It was hard, and I tried hard. I wonder how much more I would have gotten out of it, aside from exercising, if I'd done it with more courage.

The reliance on alcohol as a numbing agent to deal with my anxiety, even during times when I felt as if I was handling my mental health issues reasonably well, is one of the main reasons why I decided to quit drinking entirely. Being sober has forced me to tackle anxiety head-on, to not take the easy way out by grabbing a beer out of the fridge or pouring Kraken into a tumbler with caffeine-free cola. The other reason I stopped consuming alcohol was to avoid aggravating my heart condition, which continued to ratchet up my anxiety.

After the catheter ablation in London, I never had an episode of SVT again, but as I've gotten older, I've had an increasing amount of premature ventricular contractions. Skipped heartbeats (they aren't skipped heartbeats; they feel that way). What I've learned from having to deal with PVCs daily, some days thousands of them, is that you can have health anxiety—an irrational worry about symptoms or worrying about health without any symptoms at all—even when you truly have a physical illness. One does not help the other. I have a real heart issue (we don't know what the root cause is yet, even after a few years of tests), and, at the same time, I worry about my heart constantly. I feel every single irregular heartbeat. I've trained myself to notice my heartbeat; having SVT was good practice for that. The irony is that the more I worry about my skipped heartbeats, the more I get. And if I worry enough that I bring a panic attack on? I've landed at the emergency room three or four times, conservatively, in the last few years. I've done my best to circumvent PVC attacks by avoiding anything that can bring them on or make them worse. This includes drinking alcohol. I also have not touched caffeine since James was a baby. I will not eat dark chocolate. I will not have anything that could potentially cause an irregular heart rhythm.

When people hear how strict I am with what I eat and drink, they say, "Dave, you're so healthy!"

The reality is that I'm out of shape, and yeah, maybe avoiding all those things is technically healthy, but mentally, I know that it's not healthy in the slightest. It's avoidance. It would be dumb to drink five cups of coffee, but having one would probably be fine. And the thing that is probably best for my heart is exercise, but because *I* feel exercise makes my heart worse, I avoid it out of fear. That is not healthy. Objectively, I know that anything can exacerbate my heart condition because, really, anxiety is doing it. Not exercise. Not caffeine. Not chocolate. Not alcohol. My old friend anxiety. And as anxiety built up around my PVCs, and as the PVCs got worse and worse, which is something that can happen as you age, I became a ticking time bomb, with the potential for *anything* to set me off. I weakened a nervous system I'd been trying my best to build back up for years, and my mind and body were waiting for that one thing—whatever it might be—to break me all over again.

Who knew that it wouldn't be a heart condition that would break me but rather a broken heart?

Let's get the undiagnosed heart condition out of the way first. We can do that relatively quickly. If I share a few experiences related to my heart to illustrate its impact on me over the last several years, you can extrapolate from them some unassailable truths: my heart is temperamental, the condition is ever-present, and it's really exhausting. It's hard to explain how consistent worry breaks your body and mind and makes them vulnerable to the kind of profound breakdowns that I've had in my life. But the best thing you can do, which I have tried to get better at, is recognize when worry is headed in that direction and address it. I had a huge flare-up of PVCs in the summer of 2023, so much so that it landed me in the emergency room at Grace Hospital. I know I have a heart issue, but I also know that my mental health conditions should be of greater concern, and so before I called my cardiologist, I emailed my psychiatrist.

I could've seen it coming. It's odd that I didn't, considering how in tune I am with my body. It's impossible not to be in tune with your body when you scan it every minute. I'd just started playing basketball again and was still playing hockey on Sunday nights. That meant I was getting more exercise than I had in years. I was shooting around at the YM/YWCA with a bunch of younger guys every other night and was pleasantly surprised to discover that I was not embarrassing myself. I'd turned into a wily vet but could still shoot the rock. Do the kids still say that? My ego had been bolstered enough that I started to play once a week at a gym across the city with guys my age or older. I had designs on joining a men's league again, after having "retired" from basketball years ago. It was going to be my triumphant comeback. We'd start by playing three-on-three half-court, then add guys and run full-court, five-on-five. On the last night I played, one, *just one*, sensation in my chest ended my basketball ambitions. I ran up the court after a turnover and felt pressure on my chest as if somebody were lightly pressing it with their hands. I stopped running, told a guy who was sitting off to take my place, and walked off the court. I changed my shoes, pulled on my sweats, left the gym, and never returned. It was likely nothing. I know that now. I knew that hours later, that same night. But that monster on my shoulder whispered to me, "You were about to have a heart attack," and I listened to it, no matter how hard I'd been working to ignore it.

Not long after, when Cole was twelve and playing A1 hockey, the team had a "parents vs. kids" game halfway through the season. The previous year, my buddy Rusty and I had dominated the game. He got eight goals, and I got eight assists. I was ready for a repeat, but the feeling I'd gotten while playing basketball lingered at the back of my mind. I put on my pads and stepped onto the ice, but it was almost as if I was waiting for something to happen. Sure enough, shortly after the game started, I was skating up the ice when I felt the same kind of pressure in my chest. I skated slowly for the rest of the game, coasting around the rink in what would have amounted to a slow jog if I'd been in runners, and I have never played any sort of hockey game again.

That bothers me. It bothers me that I have continually given into fear. But more than that, it bothers me that I've missed so much time with my kids. Not only with Cole but also with Lauren, who played hockey during the two years following the pandemic, and James, who caught the hockey bug in 2022 and is presently obsessed with the sport (he's a goalie, speaking of anxiety). "Parents vs. kids" games are a part of the fabric of youth hockey in Canada. Each time since that game with Cole, my kids have asked if I was going to play, and each time, I've made up excuses about why I wasn't. One of the reasons I used was that my equipment had been left in a flooded basement and got mouldy, so I had to throw it out. I remember feeling relieved when I went to grab my hockey bag before a "parents vs. kids" game and found my equipment ruined. It also meant that I couldn't play on Sunday nights unless I invested in new equipment. One year, when Cole was fourteen and playing AAA, I opted to be the timekeeper rather than play in the game. All the parents were out on the ice with their kids, except for me; I was in a little box by myself, working the clock and updating the score. What was worse about it was that by then, Cole didn't expect me to play. Maybe it was a way that he could avoid disappointment. Maybe he was disappointed anyway and didn't say anything; Cole isn't one to talk about his feelings.

The first time I went to the hospital in a long while was after one of Cole's hockey games, the same year he played A1, during the second half of the season. I'd been feeling fine. I was in the middle of a stretch when I had relatively low anxiety. I rushed to the game from a meeting and didn't eat supper, but that wasn't a big deal, though I do like to eat at particular times, or I start freaking out. There was a sushi place close by. It was February, still cold out, but I walked to the restaurant, ordered my usual— an avocado roll and an AAC roll—and took the meal back to the rink, eating it in the stands. It was a close and intense game; back then, I was a loud parent. I liked to cheer. I wasn't the kind of parent you'd find on a viral video punching the glass, but I got into it more than if I were watching a Jets game. In the third period, I noticed my chest feeling funny. My heart was fluttering more than usual. By the time the game was over, my heart was beating hard and skipping a lot. Parents were gathering in the lobby, waiting for their kids, and I tracked Jill down and told her I needed to go to the hospital. She was unconcerned, and responded casually, like "Okay." It's not that she didn't care, it's just that she'd been through it before. More times than either of us could count. This was routine for her. Trust me, if Jill felt there was something to worry about, she would've gotten me to the hospital quicker than an ambulance. We had arrived in different cars, so she would take Cole home and I'd bring myself to the ER.

I walked to my van, got inside, and didn't wait for it to warm up; I just put it in drive and started on my way to Victoria General. I tried to quell an oncoming panic attack by belly breathing. In through the nose for five seconds, out through the mouth for seven seconds. I can feel when a panic attack is coming. It originates in the pit of my stomach. It is an escalating buzz that spreads throughout my body just like blood through my veins. It makes me feel frozen, even though I can move. The breathing didn't work, but I was close enough to the hospital that I made it without incident, parked, and walked into the emergency room. From there, everything happened the same way it had happened before, and I knew that it would. I knew it, but still, I chose to ignore each opportunity to turn around and just go home. They took my blood pressure and pulse, hooked me up to an ECG, drew blood, gave me lorazepam, and then I waited for an hour or so to see a doctor. The doctor told me that I hadn't had a heart attack, that I was fine, and then sent me off, advising me to follow up with my cardiologist. In short, I hadn't really needed to go to the hospital.

I try to set goals for myself. It's an informal practice. I think of the scariest things in my life, name them, and then try to overcome them. I fear heart palpitations. But how can I overcome this fear without eliminating or drastically reducing the palpitations themselves—something that will come only from a proper diagnosis and effective treatment? Even so, since my PVCs get worse the more I worry about them, overcoming the fear is important. The clearest outward expression of fear when it comes to my irregular heartbeat is a trip to the emergency room. Have I stopped calling 9–1–1? Yes. That's a small victory. Have I stopped going? Not really. There may have been an occasion where I was tempted to go and didn't, but typically I give in, get in the car, and drive myself to the emergency room. Is it an emergency if you can take yourself to the hospital? Likely not.

I fear heart palpitations despite evidence to the contrary. It's hard to accept that PVCs are benign. When you're in the middle of an attack, you cannot possibly think, "Oh, these are just uncomfortable, but I'm going to be okay." Trust me, it's rare. I am still committed to never googling symptoms on the internet, and I haven't—it's one of the goals I've set for myself that I have stuck with—but I have joined forums on Reddit with other people living with PVCs, and the things that we, as a community, are scared of, the questions we ask each other, are almost universal. The point I am trying to get to, irrespective of whether or not my PVCs are ever resolved, is to ingrain in my mind that no matter how bad they get they *will not kill me*. Yes, they are disruptive, mostly because I allow them to be. Yes, they are uncomfortable. Yes, if they go on for too long, I feel light-headed and dizzy and I get pale. But they are not going to kill me. My doctor and cardiologist and emergency room nurses and Jill and a bunch of other people have all assured me of that, and regardless of whether I was right about the SVTs or not, if one hundred people are telling you one thing, they are probably right. It's like on *Who Wants to Be a Millionaire.* If the "ask the audience" lifeline is used and 100 percent of the people tell you the same answer, you're an idiot if you pick a different response.

My heart began to beat irregularly again months after the incident at Cole's hockey game. By then it was spring and we'd just opened the pool. I was skimming the pool when my pulse started jumping every beat. I had an internal debate over what to do, and to my credit, I didn't go straight to the hospital but rather lay down in the family room, breathed deeply, and rode it out. After a few minutes, my heart settled, and because I wasn't done with the pool yet, I got up and started skimming it again. As soon as I stood up, my heart began to skip again. That was the pattern for the next two days. When I was on my feet, my heart began to skip every single beat. When I lay down, it resolved quickly. I was faced with a choice. Lie down for the rest of my life and enjoy a regularly beating heart or find out what was going on and see a doctor. I held out for those two days, but on the third evening, I headed to the emergency room. What grade do I get? The low or the high?

That's a bit of a trick question. There are no grades. If you begin to assign grades to your performance concerning the goals you set, you're positioning yourself to pass or fail, and it's not about that. On your journey, on my journey, you're going to have wins, and from time to time you're going to take an L. But if you're walking forward, even if you take the odd step back, you're on the path. If you set a goal and don't reach that goal immediately, there's always tomorrow. It's okay.

They kept me longer than usual at the hospital. This time I was at Grace, in St. James, closest to my house. The good thing about it, the only positive I usually find in going to the hospital, is that they caught what was happening on an ECG. They saw my heart rate when I was standing up, and they saw it beating normally when I was lying down. When they discharged me, I left with a similar experience to my previous visits, only this time I was given a prescription for metoprolol, a beta blocker. It's a medication that's used to treat blood pressure; it lowers your heart rate and it can treat PVCs. I drove to a pharmacy that was open, filled the prescription, waited around with my heart skipping the whole time, and had a pill in my mouth before leaving the store. On the way home, the PVCs resolved, and for a while they got substantially better. I thought that after years of dealing with them, of them getting progressively worse, they were finally gone.

As it turned out, the beta blockers mitigated the irregular heart rhythm but didn't resolve it. And as my body adjusted to the medication, the PVCs became more frequent again. Since then, it's been a balancing act. My doctor and I have upped the dose as high as it can safely go, and I'm sure it's helped, but things seem to work in the same way as they do with my anxiety: in waves. There are times when I hardly notice my PVCs for different reasons. They might be better one day, and then, on another day, I might be so busy that I don't have time to obsess over them. Maybe that's partially why I work so hard at this whole writing thing. The PVCs rarely bother me when I'm writing. And while I ride the undulations, the good days and the bad days, while I wait for an MRI or a CT angiogram or a stress test or a medically induced stress test because I'm too nervous to exercise on a treadmill on my own or another electrocardiogram or a bubble study, I try to repeat a mantra that helps me get through.

I'm okay, it'll be okay, this won't kill me, it just feels that way.

So, it's always there and it may always be there. Part of my treatment for the irregular heartbeats might be acceptance, which has a parallel to living with anxiety. At some point, you have to stop fighting it and accept that you have it and get on with your life.

Here's an exercise that helped me understand why acceptance is important. It was for anxiety specifically, but I think it has several applications. A therapist I saw prior to being connected to the psychiatrist I've had for most of my anxiety journey showed it to me. She had a pad of yellow Post-it notes and a pen. She took one slip of paper off the pad and wrote the word *ANXIETY* on it in block letters.

"Hold up your hand," she said.

I raised my hand, and she helped me put it in the right position—my hand stiff as a board and my arm slightly extended, as if I were motioning for somebody to stop. She then stuck the

Post-it note with *ANXIETY* written on it onto her hand and placed her hand against mine.

"Try to stop me from pushing this note closer towards you," she said, and then started to push her hand forward.

I pushed back, and it became an odd game of reverse tug of war. She pressed the note against my palm for a minute, then stopped, and took her hand away.

"That's what happens when you fight anxiety," she said. "It's hard, isn't it?"

"Yes," I said.

"Okay," she said, "now hold your hand out."

My hand was in the same position. I turned it over so that my palm was up and extended it towards her, as if I were asking for change. Then she took the Post-it note and placed it on my hand, the word *ANXIETY* facing out.

"Is that hard?" she asked.

"No," I said.

What she was telling me was that you can fight against anxiety, your mental health issues, to hold them off. But the thing is, they're already there, and there are more productive things to do. You need to start fighting in a different way. This was not an exercise to say that you should give up, but rather that you should accept what you have and fight with it, not against it. When the therapist put the note on my palm, there was no resistance. It was just there. I had it. When she pushed against my hand with the note stuck between us, I was using energy that could have been better used elsewhere.

*

I'm not perfect. Believe me. After going on beta blockers, which, as a side effect, probably helped my anxiety by lowering my blood pressure and heart rate (my heart rate never quite goes above eighty now, no matter how worked up I get—I could totally fool a lie detector test), I was now on two medications that I took twice daily: alprazolam and metoprolol. I'm still on them today: one that I need, at least until my heart issue is resolved or treated more effectively, and another that I *think* I need, and that I've become reliant on. It's not a fear of mine, taking alprazolam, but it is another goal to wean off the medication when the time is right, when I feel that I'm in a good enough place to do so, because it won't be pleasant. Alprazolam can be a highly addictive drug. One of the things my anxiety causes me to do is look at the side effects of medication and wonder which long-term impacts I will experience. I'm going to go ahead and put that on my list of things I'd like to accomplish. Get off alprazolam and on something that is less worrying and that I will take only as needed, not twice daily. I don't want to have a crutch; I want to have support, and I want to feel as though I can do this without relying on medication. On my journey, I've missed agency for too long, and agency, control over your mental health conditions, is an important thing to have.

Still, regardless of goals I had that I'd not yet accomplished, by 2019 I was in a better place. I'd settled into a manageable routine. I took my meds, I did my breathing, I did most things that my anxiety was telling me that I couldn't do, I was eating healthy and hadn't had a drink for almost two years, and I had continued my advocacy work, which had become almost as important as my work in Indigenous representation and reconciliation. I'd not even been to the hospital for a while.

I felt good about the direction in which my work was headed, too. I'd started to take my father's teaching of balance to heart and was thinking increasingly about reconciliation, that it didn't just encompass hard history and the challenges Indigenous people face in contemporary society, but that there were positive things that should be learned about and celebrated, such as cultural reconnection, language revitalization, community, and our relationship to the land. I owe this focus to Dad and the trip we took to his trapline in early summer 2018. It granted me a whole new perspective on my life, what I should be working towards, and how I might get there. I envisioned a trilogy of work that would explore the connection I had with my father, with the land, with my identity, and with my culture. That trip to Black Water, the trapline, was an anchoring point, along with my father; the glue that held everything together. All throughout 2019 I was working on a picture book called *On the Trapline*, a podcast called *Kíwéw*, and a memoir called *Black Water*. What I liked most about the work was that it brought Dad and me closer together.

By December 2019, everything was falling into place. I was halfway through recording my podcast with CBC, which was planned to be a series of five episodes, each one lasting around sixteen or seventeen minutes. I'd written *On the Trapline*, and Julie Flett, whom I'd previously worked with on *When We Were Alone*, had created beautifully serene illustrations. And I was working on a revised draft of *Black Water*. Dad had seen or read most of these projects. He'd listened to a few clips of *Kíwéw* and had read at least the prologue of *Black Water* and was pleased with it, and both Mom and Dad were in my office for my work's annual Christmas gathering when I received the first full version of *On the Trapline*, with all the words and pictures put together. I'm forever grateful that Dad was able to see it, and that he and Mom got to read it together with me.

It was the last thing I wrote that Dad got to read.

My family and I drove to Canmore that Christmas. We left on December 26, 2019, and arrived late in the evening. I'd not seen my side of the family before we left; Jill and I alternate which family we have Christmas dinner with from year to year, and in 2019, we had dinner with the Dumonts. That meant I hadn't seen my parents since a couple of days before Christmas. Dad and I had watched a football game together in the basement. Well, he watched it; I mostly fell asleep on his shoulder and was woken up by Jill when it was time for us to go home. Jill called my mother while we were driving to Alberta and my father answered the phone. She asked to speak to Mom, and my father called out, with the receiver held away from his mouth, "Bev!"

That was the last thing I heard him say.

Memories like these are tattoos.

When we arrived in Canmore, we went right to sleep. There was a full schedule the following day, starting with a walk by Jill's sister's place. Early in the morning on the twenty-seventh of December, my family, along with Dana; her husband, Martin; and their kids, Max and Jacob, walked around a field behind their house. It was a beautiful, calm stroll through unfettered snow and surrounded by mountains wherever you looked. I think about that morning a lot. I don't think I'll feel that sort of quiet in my mind again. Dad carried an ease about him that filtered into other people, and now that he's gone, that state of being is gone with him.

We visited the hot springs after lunch. I hadn't been there since I went with my grandparents when I was a kid; they took me, Michael, and our cousin Shayne on a road trip out west. The place is a gong show. There were a million people there, spread out all over the facility. We found a corner off to the side where it wasn't as hectic, and even with so many people around, it was still nice to hang out in the middle of winter in hot water on the side of a mountain with a bathing suit on. Jill and I took our phones with us and placed them off to the side where they wouldn't get wet. We hadn't been there more than twenty minutes when we got a call. I was away from my phone with one of the kids, so Jill picked it up. I watched her answer and saw her face change instantly. Within seconds, she held the phone out to me, and said, "It's your mom."

I think we have a sixth sense for bad news. For the worst kind of news. There are cues, of course. Somebody's tone of voice, even when they say something as simple as hello. And history. There's always context that reveals itself. When I look back on that moment, I can think of a few reasons why I knew, deep down, what my mother was about to tell me. Yes, it was the look on Jill's face. Yes, it was the tone of my mother's voice, the shock in it, the blankness, like everything inside had been emptied out. But there was an urgency to the work I was doing with my father, starting with when he asked me to take him to his trapline. When he asked me, sitting with me at a coffee shop by my work, his exact words were, "I want you to take me to my trapline one last time."

One last time.

I'm not naive. I knew what he meant back then. He was eighty-two years old when he asked me, he had been living with an ongoing stomach issue that nearly killed him in the early 2000s, and there was a sense he wouldn't be around for a lot longer. His question brought with it a sense of finality. It was sobering.

The simplest way to define the feeling is intuition. I remember thinking, when Jill passed me the phone, telling me that it was my mother, before I'd spoken to her and heard her voice, that *somebody* had died. The seconds between when I took the phone and when my mother talked to me, when I knew for sure, were seconds rife with the kind of mile-a-minute thoughts that are the hallmark of anxiety. I knew it wouldn't have been a family friend, because I didn't think Mom would've interrupted our short vacation for that. That meant it had to be a family member, and of course, there's no good outcome in that case. I had it in my head that it was one of my brothers, and that terrified me. It could've been Shayne or my uncle Rob or any number of other people. It's funny, though. Initially, maybe because I never wanted to entertain the possibility, or maybe because I knew it was most likely, I couldn't believe it was my father. There was so much work left for us to do. He was my father, my mentor, my best friend, my therapist, my golfing buddy, my colleague (leading up to his death, he was doing contract work at my place of employment, the Manitoba First Nations Education Resource Centre), and countless other things. But when those seconds passed, and I had the phone to my ear, and I heard Mom's voice, even before the words registered, I knew that Dad was gone.

There was no good place to receive this news, but getting it at the hot springs, in the middle of a crowd, wasn't ideal. Mom was on the phone first, telling me what had happened, which I'll keep to myself, and then, as I broke down very publicly, my brother took the phone from Mom and did his best to keep me calm. Everything's a blur for the next couple of hours, right up until my brother-in-law Martin drove me to the Calgary International Airport. The rest of that day presents itself to me in broken, non-sequitur images. Jill must've told the kids, because I was in a daze, stumbling through the hot springs and back inside the building. I remember leaning against a shelving unit to hold myself up until I got off the phone with my brother. In the change room, before Cole got there, I took an alprazolam just to make sure I didn't have a panic attack, which was bubbling near the surface. As a family, we hugged outside the building before walking to the car. Dana and Martin booked me a flight to Winnipeg from Calgary. Jill and the kids would drive back the next day. Martin got me to the airport on time, but the plane was delayed repeatedly. I sat in the same place, listening to the same music, the same songs. "Naeem" by Bon Iver. I probably listened to that song thirty times. "Requests" by John K. Samson. I don't know when the plane arrived; I wasn't paying much attention. My brain was only giving me information I absolutely needed to absorb. I cried periodically when the reality of what happened hit me. I stared blankly at the floor in shock and disbelief. People likely noticed.

People likely had no idea what to do or what was happening to me. What had happened to me. That flight, deep in the night and into the early morning, I sat there listening to those songs, staring out the window at the black and the flashing light on the tip of the plane's wing.

Michael was there to pick me up when I finally landed at two or three in the morning.

He'd brought me some food because I'd not eaten all day, since before the hot springs. We sat in the kitchen together when I got to Mom's house. Dad's house. We sat in the places we used to sit in when we were young, as though we were trying to hang on to something that wasn't there anymore. I thought of my father standing at the front door in the middle of winter, wearing his green housecoat, watching me with disapproval as I sat in the car with a girl. I thought of my father sitting in the recliner in his study listening to classical music with an old set of headphones. I thought of him eating toast with marmalade, doing the crossword with block lettering. I thought of how he liked baths, not showers. I thought of him excusing himself from company so that he could sit in the quiet in the basement. I thought of walking outside with him after I'd broken the pantry door. I thought of leaving with him to golf at Cottonwood, first thing in the morning, and how we used to stop at Robin's Donuts on the way out. I thought of a picture, of when I was a child, of sitting on his lap, of his arm wrapped around me so I wouldn't fall. I didn't understand how there wouldn't be any more memories with him, or of him. His cap was on the hook at the backdoor beside his shoes. His coat was hanging in the closet in the front hallway. There was a classical music CD in the stereo by his recliner, a pair of head-phones plugged into the stereo. There was an indent of his body, where he liked to sit, on the couch in the basement. I slept there that night when I couldn't stay awake any longer. I slept where he liked to sit. I could feel the shape of his body. I wrapped his star blanket around me and drifted away.

Dad's funeral was in January, at a church he frequently at-tended in River Heights. One of the pastors at the church hap-pens to live across from me and agreed to officiate. It was one of the last big gatherings I attended before the world shut down be-cause of COVID-19. The church was packed. That didn't surprise me. I play the game of "who would come to my funeral" because I think I'm going to die of one thing or another from week to week, and I never really know. I have a lot of friends, but not many close friends, and most of them are family, so there seems to be some sort of obligation or expectation of friendship. I've had visions of empty pews, with only my family at the front. When I'm in a better frame of mind, I picture a relatively full room. The packed house for Dad wasn't ever in question. As a minister, as a coun-sellor, as an educator, as an Elder, as a genuinely good person, he'd made a lifetime's worth of friendships, and had had an im-measurable impact on people and communities.

Following the funeral, I had some decisions to make. I still had three projects in various stages of production, all nearing comple-tion, that I needed to evaluate. But I put those decisions off until I was ready, and my publishers were amazing in their understanding. After less than two months passed, however, I felt as though I had to get back to work. Not necessarily because I was ready, but because I needed to be doing something other than grieving.

Grieving during the pandemic was an odd thing. It almost defies a meaningful description. You're stuck inside, you can't interact with people in the way you need to when you lose somebody, and you're left to your own devices. You're left isolated in your mourning. I had my family, of course, but I wasn't well-equipped to deal with the death of my father in the best way. Not that I started drinking again or anything like that, but I was lost, and there was no light to show me the way out. What's worse, I don't think I quite realized that. I thought the light would be the work, that it would keep Dad close to me, and it did. But in a way, it put off or allowed me to ignore the grieving process.

There wasn't much to do with *On the Trapline*. For all intents and purposes, it was done, and we were waiting for publication, which wasn't until 2021, on Star Wars Day, May 4. The tough decisions came with *Black Water* and *Kíwéw*. While *Trapline* was a fictional account of my trapline visit with Dad, which meant there was a layer of protection there, the other two projects were about me and my father, and I didn't think there was a way to avoid addressing his untimely death. Jennifer Lambert, my editor at HarperCollins, and I had several conversations about how to weave my father's death into the narrative of *Black Water*, but ultimately, the memoir wasn't about his death; it was about his life and our life together. So, we did some fancy editing, pulled the epilogue into the last chapter and stitched that together, and then I talked about Dad's death in a new epilogue. The rest of the book was completely unchanged, and I like the decision we made in that case. *Kíwéw* was trickier. It felt like a living document, and as such, including Dad's death in the narrative was unavoidable. I had written an outline for all five episodes, and the whole journey was supposed to be a companion piece to *Black Water*, the stuff that didn't fit into the memoir. It was an intimate, identity-centred, investigative podcast. I'd look into how and when my great-aunt died while attending a day school in Norway House Cree Nation, and where she was buried now. I wanted to figure out where my great-grandfather had been buried as well, after being admitted to the Selkirk Mental Health Centre. My producer, Julie Dupre, and I had recorded two episodes at the time of Dad's death, and when I got back into the studio to record the third episode, I'd written a different intro that addressed my father. The final two episodes became a tribute, and the challenge was to connect the last two episodes with the first three, find continuity, and make it all work.

By far the hardest, and more retraumatizing, activities surrounding these projects (once I decided to keep working on them, whether or not it was too soon) was recording them. For *Kíwéw* I had to record three episodes in early 2020, and for *Black Water* I had to read the entire memoir for the audiobook. I'd chosen to do so before my father's death, and changing my mind after he died wasn't something I was prepared to do, although I'm sure there was some conversation around that option. With the intro to episode 3 of the podcast, and the entirety of episode 4, I made it through okay. They were both done in-studio at CBC prior to the lockdown. If you listen to those episodes carefully, you'll hear my voice crack here and there, but that's something that happens when I record in the booth, for some reason, so the fact that I'm nearly crying the entire time is kind of hidden.

The audiobook for *Black Water* is another story. I spent an entire week in a recording studio, under strict protocols, reading and performing the book. My admission is that I've listened to almost none of it, only when I absolutely had to, to review a line or the pronunciation of a word. But I've heard on good authority that it's an emotional listen, and that's because I was crying half the time. Some chapters, while reading scenes that conjured a whirlwind of emotions, I knew that my voice was barely hanging on, and the epilogue, well, how do you sound when you're talking while sobbing? That's what I sound like during the last section of *Black Water*'s audiobook. The final day I recorded in the studio, which included the epilogue, I had to switch over to another studio in the same building, with the same engineer, and record the fifth episode of *Kíwéw*; CBC had piggybacked onto the session because their lockdown was so strict there was no way I was getting into their building, and recording from my home in the closet, where the acoustics would be best (I recorded a segment on the unmarked graves for CBC in my bedroom closet using an iPhone), wasn't an option because there wouldn't be consistency with the first four episodes.

It was the end of a long, emotional day, and I was exhausted physically and mentally. I'd given everything of myself for the recording—Dad deserved no less than that—and felt as though I had nothing left. My plan, upon entering the studio, was to just get through it as best I could. Initially, that meant removing all emotion to protect myself. I've never been good at self-care, but right then, I thought I needed it. I was going to insulate myself by avoiding sentiment, if that were possible, record the seventeen- or eighteen-minute episode, and get the hell out of there. I'd lie down at home, eat chips, and watch a movie or play *Fortnite* with my buddy Ryan. Something that would allow me to shut my brain off. Julie was overseeing the production remotely from the studio at CBC. Through the magic of technology (it seems like magic to me), she could listen in real-time, and communicate with me and the studio engineer in real-time as well. It was as if she were there with us. It wasn't more than a few minutes before Julie interrupted me. I was surprised at first, because technically, I'd not made a mistake yet. That was rare. I'm sure Julie has a million outtakes of me swearing into the microphone after messing up a line. What Julie told me was that I sounded too robotic. I explained to her why, but she told me that it was an emotional episode, and that I had to let those emotions out.

She may not have said it, and the engineer that I'd worked with all week may not have either, but I had a feeling that if I went there, they would support me any way they could. This had been my experience throughout the week already, so it wasn't a stretch to feel confident in that. I can't tell you how many times I stopped because I couldn't say a line through the tears. Pause. Breathe. Proceed. Pause. Breathe. Proceed. When Julie told me that I had to allow for emotions, Dad's voice popped into my head. I remembered him telling me that tears were important. Tears were a part of the healing process. "Tears are pain and grief leaving the body." For the next thirty minutes, I shed pain and grief and recorded the episode. As it turned out, I had a lot more emotion stored up.

And then it was over but for the waiting, because all those projects had yet to be published. Over the next six months, they'd be out in the world, and I would have to be out there with them. It wasn't just what I've come to call my Dad Trilogy, either; I had two other books coming out in 2020, *The Barren Grounds*, which was the first book in a middle-grade fantasy series called the Misewa Saga, and the long-planned graphic novel continuation of the Reckoner trilogy, called The Reckoner Rises: *Breakdown*. I didn't know at the time how appropriate that title would prove to be. The story is about Cole Harper again, but for me it's important that the first scene is in a therapist's office, and he's going over how the events of the first books in the Reckoner series impacted him. He begins to see things that are supernatural, and the question becomes if they're really there or if he's seeing them because of his mental health issues. I did a lot of research for the book, in depicting somebody living with post-traumatic stress disorder and the symptoms it carries. The goal was the same: that somebody would read it who needed to read it, because it reflected their lived experience. *Black Water*, too, addresses mental health challenges in a more direct way, but that theme is secondary to a trio of journeys—my father's, mine, and ours together, to his trapline.

By that stage in my career, I was used to promoting my books. I was inching closer to having published thirty books. There are always media obligations, more with one book than another, depending on the profile of the release (I did far more press, for example, for *Black Water* than I did for *Breakdown*). There are also festivals, but it was different this time around; all three of my new books were pandemic books, which meant there were no in-person festivals to attend. Everything I did in promoting my work was done virtually, in my pyjamas. I didn't (always) wear pyjamas, although it's a bonus that I had the option. I had it in my head that because I couldn't go anywhere, it would be less busy, so I took on whatever I could. That was a mistake. Without leaving the house, except for the odd time I did an event from my office at my day job because it was quiet and there weren't any kids around, I did far more events than I ever would have done had COVID-19 not happened. There are good things, albeit only a few, that have come from the pandemic. From a professional standpoint, it's expanded an artist's ability to reach their audience. The challenge is that you can become too available. That fall, when the books were released, I had multiple events every day, and I also arranged my own "Twitter Live" or "Instagram Live" sessions where I would read from one of my books and answer questions from whoever logged in. Bit by bit, hour by hour, you stretch yourself thin, and if you aren't mentally and physically well enough to cope with that, you find yourself pulled apart. People are not Stretch Armstrong toys.

And there was Dad.

He was never more present, even in his absence. I get it, that media looks for stories. I do a fair amount of freelance journalism, and I've experienced it first-hand. An angle presents itself, and media chases the story. It's their job. When *Black Water* came out, there was more of a story than there would have been otherwise because my father had died. Whoever I spoke to about the book, about my father, about our relationship, and about his death, was respectful of the fact that my family and I were grieving; it wasn't that. But it was the barrage of never-ending interviews where I had to talk about his death; that was a hard thing to do when I hadn't worked through his death myself yet. We hadn't even laid him to rest. We'd had the funeral, but not the interment.

I've never known what to make of what happened with all the events and interviews surrounding *Black Water*'s release, and *Kíwéw* as well. I always thought, and have said since, that it should've helped me grieve, to work through his loss by recalling him, the memories I had of him, and the gifts of knowledge that he gave me, the focus that has helped me in what I'm trying to do with my writing career. But grief became a fog that I couldn't see through. I was driving home with my son from Saskatoon recently, and soon after we entered Manitoba, a mist fell over the highway so thick that I had to drive half the speed limit. That's the kind of fog grief is. You can move forward, but slowly. You can see, but not that far, not much farther than within yourself. And it doesn't matter where you turn. It's there, and it stays there until it lifts, and it can feel as if it won't ever lift.

You may want to stop driving altogether.

I thought it would be cathartic to talk about my father repeatedly, that it would keep him close, and that I'd be better for it. I said as much, I acted as much, I believed as much, but the truth was that it was chipping away at me. It was chipping away at me and slowly breaking through a hardened surface I tried to create, and then digging out my insides, and one day I was empty. I guess I didn't realize just how much *Black Water* and *Kíwéw* and all the obligations around them took from me until I had nothing left to give. I think it began with my voice, in September 2020, when I had to start doing press and events. My voice, aside from my heart, was probably the thing I needed most. I may have had COVID, but the only symptom was a hoarse voice. It's odd that somebody with health anxiety didn't worry too much about COVID-19; I guess I either didn't care about getting it, what it might do to me, or I just had more important things on my mind. COVID was off in the fog somewhere, blurry and hard to see. The truth is, I think I wore myself out, and my hoarse voice was the first attempt my body made to say what it had said to me in 2010.

"You're done, Dave."

"I can't be done. I have too much to do."

The launch for *Black Water* was a beautiful event. It would've been more beautiful if I'd been able to be with people. I did the launch by myself, at night, in my office, in the dark, with only a desk lamp providing light (my low-tech way of creating a ring light, I guess). Out of all the events I've done, this was the one where I really needed somebody there with me, holding my hand. I probably didn't realize that until it was too late. There was a good turnout; people logged in from all over the country, and my dear friend Jael Richardson moderated. Having somebody safe to moderate was important to me. I knew that if I broke down, I could break down in front of her, and she could handle me breaking down. The only immediate problem was that I didn't have a voice. I watched it online afterwards, which I don't normally do, but I wanted to hear how bad I sounded; I was at least audible, and if you didn't know I had no voice, I don't think you could tell, but I was shouting the whole time to make my voice sound normal. When the launch ended, I had no choice but to give my throat time to heal, and out of necessity, not out of practice or self-care, I said no to a couple of interviews.

It was too little, too late. When the dust settled and most of the promotional activities were over for *Black Water*, the damage was done, and I was in a bad place, but it wasn't something I noticed in my mind. I didn't realize what it had done to me psychologically. Maybe I'd been so busy that I didn't have time to recognize the impact. I noticed it in my body and misinterpreted the symptoms for physical ailments. It's like I forgot that the brain could do some pretty severe things to the body, and I was feeling it all. I couldn't eat very much. I was losing a lot of weight. I felt bloated all the time, so badly some nights that I thought it was a heart issue. Speaking of my heart, the skipping had become progressively worse, to the point that I felt the skips had become regular, and my regular beats had become anomalies. Worst of all, worse even than my heart, which had always been my biggest concern, was how exhausted with life I felt. Not exhausted physically, although I certainly was, but just weary. One of my favourite books of all time is *All My Puny Sorrows*, and in it, Miriam Toews uses the term "weariness of life." For the first time in my life, with everything I had persevered through, I felt as if I was just . . . done. It was the enormity of my mental health journey weighing on me, and not so much what I had already been through but what lay ahead. I'd been told repeatedly that since there was no cure for anxiety and depression, what I was feeling, what had become the "new normal" in my life, was something I would feel for the rest of my life. The thought of that was incredibly discouraging. Immeasurably draining. And losing my father pushed it all over the edge.

I've heard the saying that once your father dies, you become a man for the first time. I don't know what happened to me when my dad died, but I do not think that it made me a man. Rather, it shattered me, and the thought of feeling the way I felt then when I was fifty, sixty, seventy, or older was something I wasn't interested in. That was probably the scariest feeling, when my weariness and exhaustion overcame my fear of death.

I remember the exact moment when I felt it: *I don't want to do this anymore.*

I felt like a failure, and everything I did played into that feeling. As had been the case fifteen years earlier, I was completely lost within myself, and everything around me, including my family, was at the periphery. I tried not to burden the kids with my problems by verbalizing them, not understanding that my behaviour was affecting them even more without an explanation. But this time around, the older ones knew what was happening, and it affected them differently. In late 2020, my oldest daughter, Emily, decided that she wanted nothing to do with me. I think it was a way for her to protect herself from the pain that my absence, though I was right there, caused. I insulated myself through stories; she insulated herself through distance. But in fairness, I'd already distanced myself; she just made it official, and I deserved that, just as she deserved better. It was undoubtedly the biggest indicator to me and my family that something was wrong and something needed to change. I didn't know what to do about it because I didn't know what to do with my own issues. It was as though I'd forgotten everything I'd learned. All the tools in my toolbox had been dumped out, either because I didn't think they would work, or because I didn't want to be better.

At my lowest point, Jill made me go for a walk. My heart was bad, my legs were weak, I was drained, and a familiar refrain played in my head. I couldn't walk up the stairs without collapsing. If I couldn't walk up the stairs, there was no way I could walk down the street. Jill, however, is convincing; you cannot say no to her when she wants something of you. That applies to her wanting her friends to have a good time at Smitty's or to her wanting her husband to go outside, get some fresh air, take a short walk, and then come home. She went with me. She held my hand all the way there and all the way back. I made it. I moved my feet and pushed through the fog. When we got back to the house, I wanted to lie down in the family room and disappear inside myself once more, but she offered to order India Palace, one of our favourite places to eat, and soon I was not in the family room but instead at the dining room table, eating chickpea curry and rice. I told her I was too bloated to eat anything. She told me to finish what was on my plate, so I did.

I feel as if I've not been direct, and that's not in keeping with the spirit of what I'm trying to do here. I'm not sure why. It could be that there's a shame associated with it, that after years of struggling, I would consider dying over living, but that was the decision that lay in front of me. That is the decision I'm faced with sometimes, even now, every week. To be clear, when I said to myself that I didn't want to do this anymore, I meant that I didn't want to go on living. When you are in a state of depression, which I had fallen into from my anxiety and other mental health conditions, from how grief had consumed me to the weariness I felt, in a desperate moment, because it can be only a moment, you *must* find something to hang onto. An anchor for me has been my children. Recently, somebody posted a question on social media. To paraphrase, the question was something like, "What keeps you here?" Meaning, what keeps you here on earth and prevents you from leaving earth for wherever you go when this life is over?

A friend wrote that their children kept them here, and I replied, "Same." I want to watch them grow up, even in my most profound depression. I don't want to miss the tiny moments that bring me interludes of joy. And because of what my father has been to me in my life, and because I know what losing him did to me, I want them to have me. Me and all my warts. They deserve, as well, to have more than just a shell of me, and so the day my wife made me go for a walk, the day she made me finish my plate of food, when faced with the decision of life or death, I chose life. Up until now, I have made the same choice for the same reasons.

Though my children are a consistent anchor, other things give me the motivation and strength to carry on. Like the saying in the notebook that Dad left behind: "I am only one, but still I am one." It reminds me that I have work left to do, and if I leave now, my work will not get done. There are more sayings than that, and I have found them helpful on my mental health journey. They are affirmations that I have come to understand as mindfulness. This one was in my father's last notebook as well:

Just for today I will not worry.
Just for today I will not be angry.
Just for today I will be grateful.
Just for today I will do my work honestly.
Just for today I will be kind to every living thing.

They are reiki intentions and principles, and what they say to me is exactly what I often need to hear but fail to listen to. Just for today, I'm going to ignore all those little monsters and live the way I want to live, the way I wish I could live, and see what happens.

Dad died in December 2019, right after Christmas. It wasn't until 2022 that I tried golfing, which was my thing with Dad. It was one of the foundations of our relationship. We spent hours, and walked miles, on golf courses. At the time of his passing, I still had never beaten him, except for one round where he was sick, and I don't have the heart to count that as a win. It was a win with an asterisk, maybe. We tied the last game we played together. It felt wrong golfing without Dad, almost as if I was acknowledging his death and moving on from him. But then I realized it was the opposite, especially when I got to golf with my son Cole. I wanted him to remember golfing with me like I remembered golfing with my father.

I went to John Blumberg Golf Course with Cole and my brother-in-law Martin, and we golfed the front nine. There were no power carts available, so we could either wait ten to twenty minutes to see if a power cart came in, or we could walk. If we chose to wait, there was a good chance we wouldn't get nine holes in before dark. If we went out right then, we would almost certainly finish. Here's the thing: I had it in my head that if I walked, it would set off my heart, and without a cart, I'd be stuck without a quick route to the hospital. Golf courses, even the relatively flat Blumberg, have hills and valleys, and walking up them is like climbing stairs. We all know how I feel about stairs. To make matters worse, I'd have to use a pull cart weighed down with golf clubs. The voice whispering in my ear was telling me to wait. It was much safer to wait. I'd live if I only just waited.

I thought of my father, and of how Cole would remember the round. Cole's been around for a few of my panic attacks, and I've neglected his worry in favour of my own self-involvement. I didn't want him to worry about his father; I wanted him to have fun playing golf with his old man.

I decided that we would walk, and I didn't let Martin and Cole know how scared I was. On the first hole, I played terribly. I was preoccupied. I was focusing on my heart. I was rushing so that we could finish sooner and get it over with. I walked down the fairway, taking three shots to Cole's one, and had a conversation with my anxiety that went something like this.

"Your heart is skipping like crazy right now," the little monster said. "Do you feel it?"

Feeling my pulse is almost as bad for me as googling symptoms. I try not to do it, but I'm hyper-aware of irregular heart rhythms anyway. I knew that my heart was skipping as much as an old, warped record under a dull needle.

"Yeah, I can feel it," I said.

"You might pass out by the time you get to the second tee," the little monster said.

"You're right; that could happen," I said. "But you know what else could happen?"

"What's that?" the little monster asked.

"Nothing," I said. "I mean, what if everything works out? What if my heart settles down, and I have a good time?"

"Fuck you," the little monster said.

"Fuck you, too," I said.

My heart skipped prominently for the better part of three holes, but then a funny thing happened. Halfway through the third hole, I stopped noticing my heart as much, it stopped skipping as much, and I played the rest of the round without allowing fear to control me. The first two holes, I'd shot an eight, the dreaded snowman, and a five, a double bogey on an easy par three, respectively. I was down by three or four strokes, and I had a long way to go if I was going to give Cole a challenge. For the next six holes, I parred four, and I bogeyed two. By the time we reached the ninth tee, it was a close match between all three of us. I was up by one on Cole and two on Martin. I made a mess of the ninth hole, I'm going to be honest, but I had a putt to win (for a double bogey, but who needs to know that?).

The point was that I had made a choice. Every day, we're faced with several choices when it comes to mental health issues. We face something, or we run from it. Choices have outcomes that are positive or negative. I chose to think of my father in a good way and to golf with my son so that we would both have memories to cherish, like Dad and I cherished memories we shared on the course. (I also beat Cole, which feels right.) I walked an entire nine holes, and it reminded me of the trip I took to Superstore years earlier when Jill made me grocery shop. I didn't think I could do it, but with every step and every shot I took, I felt better and more confident. I came home that evening having had a great time and knowing that if carts weren't available next time, I didn't have to freak out about it. In fact, maybe I'd even choose to walk.

Just for today I will not worry.

From that point on, after the walk and a plate of Indian food, I made the choice to go on a journey of rediscovery, not self-discovery. It was the mantra of "Just for today . . ." but repurposed. Personalized.

Just for today I will get out of bed and take a walk.
Just for today I will listen to music that I love.

Just for today I will eat three meals even if I don't feel like it.
Just for today I will give myself grace.
Just for today I will be more present in the lives of others.
Just for today I will be here for tomorrow.

A lot of things helped when I made the decision to heal rather than permanently disappear into the pain. For example, I decided to stop listening to my father's voice, of which I had hours of recordings, to torture myself. During the bad period, I sat in my car in the driveway listening to the same clip of him talking fifty times in a row and invited tears from my grief. I didn't hear what he was saying; I just lamented that this was all I'd ever have of him. Rather, I started to listen to my father's voice so that we could continue to develop our relationship even though he was physically gone, and I could keep learning from him. There is so much in his words that teaches me about myself, about the world I am living in and how I can contribute to making it a better place. But I cannot do that if I am not around, and I have to take steps to protect myself.

Christopher Priest wrote in *The Prestige*, "I planned to waste away and die, but there is a spirit of life, even in one such as myself, that stands in the way of such decisions."

The decision to keep fighting, to keep living, is not passive. You don't lie in bed and wait for that one thing to change, to wake up and notice that the sun is shining a little brighter. If you wait it out, just trying to make it one more day while doing the same things you were doing before, you will not get to where you need to be to continue to, or start to, heal. You have to actively decide that you want to make it one more day, and you're going to, just for today, do everything in your power to get to the next day.

The activities surrounding that decision can differ for people in some ways, and not in others. For example, music started to play a big role in my healing, in my ability to see the light shine a bit brighter, a little at first, and then more consistently. You may not get there by listening to Bon Iver and John K. Samson and Taylor Swift and the National and Sufjan Stevens. In fact, some of that music may be a bit of a downer to some people. I've always appreciated beauty in music and the stories music can tell, and knowing that stories in any form can heal. But hey, "Party in the USA" is absolutely a song that can cheer somebody up. I love that song. My mother might choose to listen to "Tiny Bubbles" by Don Ho or something by Nana Mouskouri. Who knows? The point is that listening to a song that brings something out of you other than emptiness is listening to a song that is worth being heard. The songs that helped me through the night my father died were the same songs that helped save my life when the chips were down and I was ready to give up.

I wanted to be more present in my children's lives. I wanted them to know that their father was there for them in the most important ways. Not that I provided for them so that they could go to school or play sports or get a treat now and then, or get clothes, or whatever. To just be there. To just be present. Truly present. Not just be in the room where they are but make some popcorn, sit with them, put my arm around them, and watch a movie with them. A line in *Guardians of the Galaxy Vol. 2* essentially says that a father isn't the same as a dad. I needed to be a dad. And that decision helped to heal my relationship with Emily, whom I'd been estranged from for months. One night, she needed a ride from a friend's house and asked me to pick her up, or maybe I was the only one available, but either way, she was ready to talk to me. So I got in the car, and I picked her up. On the way home, she explained why she hadn't been speaking to me and told me she was ready to rebuild our relationship. We talked all the way home, and since then, for the most part, we've been good despite the odd bump in the road in any parent/child relationship. Better than good. Emily's one of the best friends I have. The trials that are put in front of us have been presented to us for a reason, and if we can push through them and learn from them, we come out the other side better for it. Emily and I would not be as close as we are today if we hadn't been through what we went through, a trial that I take full responsibility for but that we both have benefited from. And the kids generally, I think, would say that they noticed a shift.

I'd put off antidepressants on several occasions in the past. In 2010, when things were at their worst, my doctor suggested that I go on antidepressants—selective serotonin reuptake inhibitors, or SSRIs—to help me out during my breakdown. I wasn't interested in trying that type of medication; I'd heard enough horror stories about it. Even if it eventually helped, I'd probably have to go through two weeks or more of hell as my body adjusted to the meds. "Here, take some meds to deal with the meds" seemed like a counterintuitive way to deal with the side effects that I felt were inevitable. My thoughts spiralled to what felt more like a comedy skit. "And then we have these meds to deal with the meds that help cope with the other meds." This was around when my doctor told me that I couldn't magically change how I think. But, I wondered, if the problem was the way my brain worked, why couldn't I change that without meds? It was rudimentary. They were right, though. You cannot change the way you think overnight. It takes work. I've always said to new and emerging writers that you cannot get to where I am, where a lot of my colleagues are, without hard work. Hard work, above all else, above even skill, gets most of the credit for what I do. The same's true here, and since change requires an investment of effort and emotional and mental labour, I suppose it makes sense that there should be a buffer. Take something like mindfulness, which in theory sounds great, but in practice is very hard. What's mindfulness? It's a form of meditation. My problem is that my brain never stops, it never gives me a break, so how am I supposed to meditate? How am I supposed to find that sort of focus? I still haven't quite figured that out. I've tried, but, admittedly, I've given up too fast.

Don't give up too fast. If you don't, I'll give it another try, too. We're in this together, right? The focus of mindfulness is an awareness of self, of what you're feeling in the moment. Not in the past, not in the future (that's what makes it so hard for anxiety warriors). *Now.* But you're supposed to just be aware. That's it. Don't judge it. Don't try to dissect it (which I always do). Just sit with it, breathe, and sometimes use guided meditation. It's a discipline, and while you're growing in that discipline, you may need something to bridge the gap. I was too afraid of the side effects of medication when I was younger. I'd gone and picked up a prescription. I held a white pill in the palm of my hand. But I couldn't pop it in my mouth. I guess it shows how bad it got that in 2020, I finally managed to take an antidepressant.

Back in 2010, fourteen years ago, my doctor felt that an SSRI was necessary to help "rewire" my brain, to allow it the opportunity to heal itself without the intrusion of my mental health conditions. My brain needed a break. But I wasn't necessarily depressed back then. I thought I may have been at the time, but falling into depression in 2020 made me realize that I had been nowhere close to depressed before. And so, in the dark days following my father's death, the SSRI was not prescribed to rewire my brain from a nervous breakdown or crippling anxiety; it was literally to help save my life. I had no interest in living the way I was living, the way I had been living, and the way I thought I was going to keep on living. I just didn't have any fight left in me. And that's what it had felt like for over a decade. A fight. I'd won some rounds, lost some rounds, and now my legs were rubber, and I could barely stand. I was Apollo Creed against Drago, only in this iteration, I begged Rocky to throw the white towel.

Suicidal ideation is no joke. There's a river by my house. I used to walk down the street close to it and imagine myself walking into the cold water and being swept away. I had a bottle of alprazolam, which helped numb my anxiety. What would happen if I just poured the whole thing into my mouth? Driving alone on the highway or a desolate stretch of road in the city, why didn't I turn my wheel to the side and hit a pole? I have these thin scars on my arms if you look closely. When nobody was in the house, or when nobody was awake, I'd hold a razor blade to my skin, press down, and watch a stream of red blood navigate my arm hair, collect at my elbow, and drip into the sink. At any moment, I could have descended the riverbank. I could have emptied that yellow bottle. I could have jerked my wheel to the right and hit a pole without hurting anybody else. I could have pressed a little harder. It was scary to think that way, and I knew I wouldn't stop feeling that impulse without help. So, one night, as I sat with an antidepressant tablet resting on my palm, I raised it to my mouth, let it tumble down my tongue towards my throat, and swallowed it.

It was a choice. I had a choice. There is always a choice. I won't get into selfishness or the people who will miss you or lay any guilt trip. I did that all to myself. I still do from time to time. But you have to know that if you make it one more day, you do not know what tomorrow will bring for you. And if whatever you're imagining doesn't come tomorrow, why not stick around for another day? If you're thinking the same thing I was thinking, does it really matter if you hang on a bit longer? You may find that one thing that encourages you to stick around, because you matter.

I watched this TikTok video recently. The smallest things sometimes help me. The smallest things, the biggest things. It was a kid who randomly went to a house that had one of those camera doorbells. Let's give credit where credit is due: thirteen-year-old Jacksen Proell, in the summer of 2023, was with friends who wanted to play ding-dong-ditch (something most of us have played). Jacksen had other designs. In the clip, he approaches a house, rings the doorbell to trigger the camera, and says, "You matter, alright? There's always going to be somebody who cares about you. And you're a good person. No matter what people say, you matter . . . keep that in mind, don't forget that."

Keep that in mind. Don't forget that.

First, we need more kids like Jacksen in this world. Second, he is right. Sometimes, you may not feel that way, but it's your little monster telling you that, lying to you. That's the voice you need to ignore. That's the voice I had to learn to ignore. When I passed by the river, I stopped imagining walking into it and started to imagine myself sitting by it, on one of those park benches, watching a pelican standing on a rock in the middle of the swift water, and letting calm wash over me. When I drove down a desolate stretch of road in the morning in the winter, I didn't think about swerving to the left but rather looking to the right, admiring a sun dog hovering over the trees, and thinking to myself how glad I was that I got to see that. The little monsters get beat by the smallest things.

And there was Story.

I've said it a million times since I started to pursue this dream of mine to become a writer. Art saves lives. I know because it helped save mine. Art in all its forms. Music, of course. I have no idea where I would be if it weren't for music. It got me through the death of my father, both acutely, the day he died, and afterwards, when I was working through, struggling through, the grief of his loss. "Requests" by John K. Samson. I'm lucky to have John as a friend. We went for coffee the other day, and as we were sitting outside a coffee shop in Winnipeg, I was able to tell him that his music, and that song in particular, helped me during the hardest time in my life. I have an entire playlist for every book I write. I have a playlist for when I feel sad and I want to cheer up, or if I want to feel sadder, because it's important to feel your emotions if you can do that safely. Don't run from them, because if you do, you may want to numb them out in negative ways. There's also dance, movies, television, painting, and photography. The best photo I ever took was of my father on our way to his trapline. I snapped the picture with my grandfather's old Kodak Vigilant Six-20. There are so many settings on that camera, and the boat was so rocky, that the photograph of my father had no business turning out like it did. But it's clear, it's gorgeous, and it gives me a father that I remember the most. Calm. Strong. Proud. Quiet. Thoughtful. I have that picture as my desktop wallpaper. I use it during lectures sometimes. I tell teachers or business professionals that it's a part of the story I'm telling, but really, it's to have him with me, to make sure he's looking over my shoulder, helping to guide me.

Bill Murray tells a story about a painting that saved his life. Before he found success as an actor, he was depressed and thinking of ending his life. He was wandering the streets of Chicago one night, thinking of dying by suicide, and found himself in the Art Institute, staring at a painting called *The Song of the Lark*. The painting is of a girl holding a sickle and taking a break from work in a field. Murray says, "I thought, 'Well, there's a girl who doesn't have a whole lot of prospects, but the sun's coming up anyway, and she's got another chance at it.' So I think that gave me some sort of feeling that I, too, am a person, and I get another chance every day the sun comes up."

One more day.

Stories heal.

I've written stories for countless reasons, but whatever the reason, the sum of my intention is healing. Representation is a pathway to healing. The stories I write are stories that I often see myself reflected in, as well. Even when I don't think my life experience is mirrored in a story I write, I find that it is if I dig deeper. A graphic novel like *Will I See?* was not my original concept; it came from my friend Iskwé and her cousin Erin Leslie. It's a story about a girl who finds relics from other women and girls who have been murdered or gone missing while walking home one day and eventually is targeted herself. She fights off the assault. It was my first foray into pulp horror with graphic novelist G.M.B. Chomichuk. An animated version served as a music video for "Nobody Knows," a song Iskwé wrote following the murder of Tina Fontaine in Winnipeg, Manitoba. What does that have to do with a forty-something-year-old guy? I have three Cree/Métis daughters, and their safety is a concern of mine. Any father with a daughter is concerned for their girl's safety, but in Canada, Indigenous women, girls, and Two-Spirit people are far more at risk than any other segment of the population. Writing that story reflected my fear as a Cree father of Indigenous girls. When Emily didn't call us once when she took a bus to her swim practice, or when our middle daughter Anna got lost at the St. James Civic Centre, Jill and I felt a fear that only an Indigenous parent can feel. I cannot lie and will tell you that killing off the antagonist in *Will I See?* and how it was done was empowering on many levels.

Some stories are more personal.

Black Water is a memoir, and you cannot get more personal than that. I'm the protagonist, and it's about my life, everything that came before me, everything that is around me now, and everything that is yet to come. If you flip the mirror around, however, *Black Water* is a story that other people, Indigenous and non-Indigenous alike, have seen themselves reflected in, for primarily two reasons: they have lost a parent, or they are living with mental health issues like I am. It is so meaningful to me that they feel inclined to approach me in person or contact me online. Either is fine and welcome. When I was starting to climb out of the deepest and darkest hole in 2020, following the loss of my father, and my body and mind had given out for the second time, stories came back again to help me heal. They came in the form of music. They came in the form of a comic strip that illustrator Scott B. Henderson, my frequent collaborator, made. I don't know where he learned it from, but I found a scene that at least retells it on *West Wing*. A guy gets trapped in a hole and can't get out. Soon, a doctor walks by, and the guy calls out for help. The doctor writes a prescription, throws it into the hole, and then keeps walking. There is nothing the guy in the hole can do with the prescription. Next, he hears somebody else walking by, and it turns out it's a priest. He calls out for help, and the priest tells the man he'll say a prayer, and then keeps walking. God never helps the guy out of the hole. Finally, a stranger, a normal person, walks by. Not a doctor. Not a priest. The trapped guy calls out for help, and the stranger climbs into the hole with him. The guy says, "Why did you do that? Now we're both trapped down here." The stranger says, "Yeah, but I've been down here before, and I know the way out."

There was something my father told me before he passed away. We were on Black Water, one of the traplines he grew up on. He told me that while he spent a lot of time on Black Water, it was a gathering place where families from different traplines came together before going off onto their own tracts of land. My father spent more time on another trapline, but one that had become lost. He couldn't remember exactly where it was; even the guide who brought us out onto the land didn't quite know. He had an idea, but the waterway had become so thin that a motorboat couldn't get there. We'd need to get there with a canoe. That would be difficult. Getting to Black Water was difficult, and if the guide was right about where the other trapline line was, it was about fifteen kilometres farther away. I had a plan, though. Like the adventures I'd written about in the Misewa Saga, I wanted to go on a quest. Only on Earth, up north, to where my father grew up. I have found that stories are incredible for another reason—we go to the places we read about, even if they are on another planet. In another dimension. Or up north. When my father told me about this lost trapline, I decided I would get there, one way or another. That was the seed.

When I decided that I was going to write about my experience with anxiety and depression, that seed became the framework for a story; it would be what you may call, albeit loosely, a MacGuffin, because there is a purpose to it, just not the main purpose. Then, I took all the things I'd been through that had thrown me into depression, all the consequences of being trapped like I was, all the things that helped me out of my depression, and developed a plot.

There's a guy named Matthew who has dealt with a feeling of loss and emptiness his entire life. There is a hole in him that he tries to fill with damaging things. The only real anchor he sees is his father; he neglects to see how his daughter and wife are anchors, too. His despondency leads him to an estrangement with his daughter, Holly, who is going through what Matthew is going through, but he can't see it. He can't see through his own despair. When his father dies, Matthew decides that he's going to bring the ashes to a lost trapline, and Holly, seeing an opportunity where her father has to be with her, goes with him. The journey to the trapline becomes a journey back to themselves and back to each other. I called it *The Theory of Crows*, based on the concept that crows remember faces and can pass down that recognition intergenerationally. What if, just like we remember the people and places that have come before us, the places our ancestors have been remember us? It's a beautiful concept. *Crows* is a novel that pays tribute to Story, to music, to the land, to family, to fathers and daughters, and to the journeys we take, no matter how difficult they might be, to get to a place where we understand ourselves better, where we accept ourselves more, and where we understand that if we get trapped in a hole, we can find our way out. More than that, we can get into the hole with somebody else and guide them out, too.

Maybe someone can hear our voice in their ear, instead of the voice of the little monsters on their shoulders.

Matthew finds his way home, which made me realize I could do the same. *The Theory of Crows* is a work of fiction, but it's fair to call it autofiction. The good old internet says autofiction combines narrative forms: autobiography and fiction. A writer recounts their experiences in the third person, and modifies what they like by altering details, adding subplots and imagined scenes, and blending all that together with experiences, places, and people in their real life so they can better understand who they are and better articulate how they got there. Holly is named after a character in a string of songs by the Hold Steady: Hallelujah. Connected to *hallelujah*, *Matthew*'s biblical meaning is "gift of God." That's just some clever footwork, I suppose, but I do love the Hold Steady, and there are musical references all over the place in *Crows*. Matthew's father is my father, and just like my father still has an important presence in my life, he has an important presence in the lives of Matthew and Holly. Matthew and Holly become estranged, just like Emily and me. And having the characters seek and find the lost trapline makes me feel like, in some way, I found it myself.

I still want to go there. I still think that's a part of the journey I'm on. I am not sure where my destination is—it would be boring if I was—but I have an idea of how I can get there. I have an idea of all the little and big obstacles I need to overcome to help me get there. I have to be okay with my failures, even celebrate them, as much as I have to celebrate my successes. No matter how tough it is, no matter how awful I feel, no matter how deep that hole I'm in.

NINE
THE WOLF YOU FEED

Celebrating failures means that you're alive to do so. I am not always grateful for just being here, but I try to remember that I should be. There are a few messages I listen to repeatedly from varied sources, from social media clips to movie speeches to song lyrics. I try to not only hear them but listen to them and ingrain them so that even on the days when I face something and give in to my fear, it doesn't lead me to the place that I was in 2010 and again in 2020.

I try to remember that I am alive against incredible odds. Neil deGrasse Tyson talks about this in a clip I've seen on TikTok, but it probably exists elsewhere as well. He lays out a purely scientific argument for the miracle of existence. I am not a math guy. I never was, and I never will be, so I won't try to explain how he came to this number—I wouldn't understand it anyway—but he says that the chances of you being alive are something like one in a million trillion trillion, and that might be underestimating the odds. What does that mean? It means that me being on this planet is so far beyond winning the lottery that I can't even wrap my head around it. I've had a similar thought before, although not in such a scientific way. I've thought to myself, and forgive how indelicate this is, *Out of how many millions of sperm did I find a way to the egg?* Not even that, but out of all the times over all the years that those little swimmers went to waste, I'm here. Is that not a gift?

Sometimes, I have moments of clarity where I can connect all these messages. When I think about the fact that my being here is a miracle, I consider that everything that happens in my life is a part of that miracle, like it or not. In 2019, Stephen Colbert spoke about grief with Anderson Cooper. Both have suffered the same kind of loss that many of us have: loss of a parent, loss of a sibling, loss of somebody we dearly love. In an interview with *GQ* magazine years before, Colbert had talked about the death of his father and two brothers when he was ten and stated that he had learned to love the thing he most wished had not happened. Anderson read that quote back to him and asked if he really believed it. Colbert said that he did, and he'd learned this because it is a gift to exist. That doesn't mean that he wanted the worst thing in his life to have happened. I certainly didn't want my father to die. But if you're grateful to be alive against such insurmountable odds, then you must be grateful for everything life throws at you. "You have to be grateful for all of it," Colbert said. There is no scenario in which you are grateful to be alive but grateful only for select moments. It's all or nothing. He goes on to talk about exactly what I feel the power of Story is, and that is that gratefulness stems from the awareness of another's pain, by experiencing your own pain. For example, I lost my father, and I want my father beside me right now, but losing him has fostered so many connections with others who share similar grief, which, Colbert says, "allows you to love more deeply and to understand what it's like to be a human being."

Lived experience. Reflection. Connection. Community.

I have obstacles, and so do you. We may share obstacles; we may not. Some of you may have sterling mental health in your life, and that's great. We connect in different ways. We certainly share the necessity to learn how to overcome those obstacles, whatever they are. Loss. Anxiety. In the case of mental health challenges, there are also differences. I live with depression and health anxiety, primarily. You may have agoraphobia, obsessive-compulsive disorder, or post-traumatic stress. You may not live with mental health conditions but know somebody who does, a friend or a family member, and reading about somebody else's struggles may help you to understand the struggles of those close to you. Trust me, people who live with mental health issues appreciate being seen and understood.

I have learned that the more you listen to anxiety, or any mental health challenge, the bigger it gets, the more it weighs you down, until you're in a hole waiting for somebody to help you out of it. A doctor. A priest. Eventually, you hope, somebody will get in the hole with you and help you find your way out. The next time, you are more equipped, and you can find your own way out. Eventually, you willingly jump into the hole to guide somebody else. That thing that grows inside of you? I've always thought of it as an entity. As a monster. A little monster at first, but one that grows into something big and scary and heavy. My therapist said that when I don't listen to the monster, it shrinks until I can carry it in a better way. I personally do not think I will ever be rid of the monster from my life, but I can carry it with me if I make it small, like a photograph in the wallet in my pocket or the spare change

I'll never use. There is an old story that resonates with me. The origins aren't clear and are often disputed, so I'm going to cut out all the religious or cultural ties and relate the tale only to mental health.

It's the story of the two wolves. It has different titles, just as it has different iterations. I call it "The Wolf You Feed." The story has two protagonists, a grandfather and a grandson. If you know my work, you know how much I like intergenerational connections, so, of course, this story speaks to me. The grandfather tells his grandson that there are two wolves fighting inside of him. This is clearly a metaphor for inner conflict of some kind. For me, it's a metaphor for anxiety and depression. I don't think life is so black and white that we can say one wolf is bad and the other is good. But I think we can say that one wolf is telling you the things you cannot do or the horrible things that you are, while the other wolf is telling you that you can do it or that you are not the awful things you believe you are. The grandson asks his grandfather which wolf wins, to which the grandfather replies, "The one you feed." It might work better generally as a bad wolf and a good wolf, but life's a bit greyer than that. Would I prefer not to have had anxiety and depression? Yes. Do I like who I am? I try to. Am I who I am in part because of the anxiety and depression that I live with, and what I've been able to fight through, those obstacles that they have presented? Absolutely.

Everybody who lives with mental health challenges has their own wolves that are fighting over different things, because the "bad" wolf has different things to say. There are particular fears that I have, things I am afraid to do, things that I'm afraid I am, that others may not have. But whatever my fears are, whatever your fears are, each of us has to overcome that fear to live in a better way. I have a mental list of fears or challenges or obstacles; whatever you want to call them is fine. There are days when I fight through them, and there are days when I don't do so well. But it helps to write them out so that I know what they are and can set goals or actions that help me work towards overcoming them (you may find this helpful, too). Fair warning: Some of these may seem silly to you, or easy, and that's okay. I totally get it. I am afraid of a few dumb things. But I'm still afraid, so I still have work to do.

I'm afraid of walking up stairs, or even up a gradual incline. This might be cheating, as it falls within the purview of exercise; however, it's on my mind so often that I felt as though it needed its own mention. Whenever I am confronted with a staircase, no matter how many steps there are, an alarm bell goes off in my brain. I start to panic. I count the stairs, which doesn't help. If it's ten steps or thirty steps, it's intimidating. I imagine having a heart attack halfway up or even just triggering my arrhythmia, which I know will not kill me, but I feel like it will, and either way, it's an awful sensation. My first instinct, after counting the number of stairs, is to look for an elevator if there are no escalators around. I've taken an elevator up one floor many times in the past. I've felt pathetic about it in each instance, but I still do it. Where am I at with it? Sometimes I suck it up, gather my courage, and take the stairs. It helps when I'm with other people who instantly take the stairs because they don't even think about it, and so what am I going to do? "Hey, guys, I'll meet you up there in a second." When I was in Hong Kong in February 2023, at the schools I visited, everybody took the stairs, and there were many, many floors. I had to take the stairs with them. I felt winded at the top. My heart was skipping after I'd made it. But I didn't die, and the palpitations eventually subsided. My goal is clear. When presented with a choice of whether to take the stairs or an elevator or an escalator, I should choose the stairs because I can do it. I know I can. And come to think of it, I have to include those automatic sidewalk things at airports, because I will always jump on one of those. I shouldn't use them. I don't need them. The only reason I should ever take them is if I need a boost when I'm late for a connecting flight. That's it. So, I've written this fear down, and with it, I've written down the actions I will take to overcome that fear.

More generally, I am terrified of exercise. This has been a problem since I first felt pressure in my chest when I was playing basketball and hockey. I have not shed one bead of sweat in years, and that's not good for several reasons. Most important, it means that I have relented to my fear at every turn, every chance I've had. I have yet to take the leap and exercise, even lightly, for a few minutes. I accidentally sweat. I have a nightmare or sleep in a hotel room where the temperature hasn't been set right, and I wake up damp. I have a panic attack or have an hour or so of bad anxiety, and my armpits get wet. None of that is exercising. It's being hot or being anxious. I'm not getting any younger. I thought of that today while walking around Amarillo, Texas, with my wife and oldest son in ninety-five-degree Fahrenheit heat, just a few blocks up and down historic Route 66. I wanted to stop, sit on a bench, and say to Jill and Cole, "It's okay, you guys go on ahead." At least I walked the same distance, but I was nervous about it, and I had this nagging dose of reality that I was approaching fifty, my body wasn't what it used to be, and I needed to be in shape if I wanted to be around for a long time (and more often than not, I do). I walked then, but earlier in the day, Jill went for a walk in a park while Cole was playing hockey, and I sat on a bench and watched her. I did some work, but mostly, I just sat on my ass. I failed, I succeeded. That's the path.

But walking isn't enough. The last two times I've had a stress test for my heart, I've been too scared to run fast enough to get my heart rate to where it needs to be for an accurate reading. The nurses and doctors blamed the beta blockers, but I knew that I was holding back. I was hooked up to machines that were literally there in case something went wrong, that would have ensured I was safe if something *did* go wrong, and I still couldn't bring myself to exercise. I had to get a medically induced stress test. They pumped me with medication that opened my arteries, which mimicked exercise, and monitored my heart for five minutes before giving me the antidote because I was crying. I was terrified of what was happening in my chest. The antidote was caffeine. It was an awful experience, and it would have been so much better if I had only run harder for five minutes on my own. I've been avoiding caffeine for years, but I had two doses of it to contract my arteries and settle my heart down. If I had a cup of coffee, I would not die.

I've written down that I'm afraid of exercise. Underneath that, I've listed steps to overcome that fear; namely, *you have to sweat, David.* Just a little bit at first. Then, gradually, a little bit more. I don't have to run a marathon right away. I just have to get on the exercise bike in the basement for a few damn minutes. If I sound frustrated, that's because this is frustrating. It's hard not to feel ridiculous about fears like this; that's something else I need to overcome. But the answers are waiting for me whenever I'm ready to go harder than the voice tells me I can.

I know that I've come a long way, and I know I won't do it all overnight, but I have a long way left to go.

I trigger my anxiety, and it can bring on a panic attack when I break my schedule. It reminds me of my daughter Lauren, who has anxiety just like me. Apparently, we also like to talk and hug a lot. Lauren likes things to happen as they are expected to. If her pépère, Jill's father, is supposed to pick her up at 7:00 a.m. on Saturday to take her out with her brother James, he has to be there at 7:00 a.m. Not 7:03 a.m. If a friend is supposed to come over at a certain time and, for whatever reason, has to bail, she has a tendency to lose it. I think these are miniature, or large, panic attacks. They're not pleasant for us, but we keep in mind that they are even worse for her. When she loses her composure, she's learned strategies that she has worked on to quell the anxiety and panic. A big one is breathing. She takes what she calls snake breaths. She breathes in, then lets her breath out so that it sounds like a snake.

Lauren is very aware of her anxiety and panic; she can articulate her emotions at a level beyond her age, and her journey is to continue to incorporate her strategies so that she can live more functionally with her anxiety. For what she has to deal with, she's done extremely well. She has a saying on her wall that encapsulates her character perfectly: "Though she be but little, she is fierce." I've noticed, also, that she has started to reason her way out of panic. A situation will present itself to her, and she talks her way through it until the panic is warded off. Maybe it's the words she says, and I think that's certainly a part of it, but I also think it's the time and distance from disappointment the talk gives her.

As for me, as I've shared, I eat at certain times of day, or else I start to worry about being hungry, about feeling weak, about feeling shaky, about how close I will have to eat to my next meal if I eat my lunch too late in the afternoon. Because I still have bloating problems, it can cause a domino effect where I eat lunch late, so I eat dinner late, and I go to bed feeling awful because I ate too close to bedtime. It's a bit more important to take medication at certain times than it is to have breakfast or lunch or supper on a schedule—and so I have a strict regimen for that. If I miss a dose, or if I can't remember whether I took one or not, I get anxiety, which can build into panic. What I have to realize in both situations—while acknowledging that one is more serious than the other—is that a little variation isn't the end of the world. If I eat breakfast late, I can eat less so that lunch doesn't have to be pushed back. If I miss my metoprolol, there's enough built up in my system that nothing awful will happen if I skip a pill and take it at the right time in the evening. I have learned self-talk from Lauren in this way (sometimes, I think she has taught me more than I have taught her). The rationalization I just wrote down on the page is the talk I try to have with myself if I miss a meal or a pill or go to bed at the wrong time or wake up too early. I'm further along in overcoming this fear than I am the others on my list. One time, I didn't realize that I'd not taken my alprazolam until it had been two hours since I should have taken it. And when I went to the trapline with my father, I forgot to take it for hours. This shows me that I can function without it, and it gives me hope that while I have gotten better at using it as a support, not a crutch, I might one day be able to live effectively with anxiety without pills. I might be able to manage things through behaviour and strategy rather than medication. After all, medication is helpful, but, the way I look at it, it is, for the most part, a bandage. The end goal is to heal, not to cover something up for a period of time.

I have a long list of fears that I live with. Honestly, there are too many to count. Everything from fear of failure to fear of bodily symptoms, which is particular to me and others like me who live with health anxiety. Some fears can be overcome with relative ease; others seem as if they can only be managed rather than overcome or cured. I need to be realistic with myself in setting goals so that I'm not discouraged by failing to reach them, even if failure is not a mark of character or lack of progress. I don't think I'll ever stop scanning my body for symptoms. It's been well over fifteen years now, and changing a way of thought that's been a part of my life for so long seems unrealistic. Maybe I can do it, but I'm not sure that I can. There are things, however, that I know I can do—or that I can stop doing, more accurately. I don't google symptoms anymore. If I feel something in my body, it might concern me, it might concern me a great deal, but I will never visit MedHelp or the Mayo Clinic website or anywhere else to search what my symptoms could be an indicator of. I'll monitor it, and if the symptoms persist, I will make an appointment with my doctor and I will ask them about it. It's important to trust that my doctor, except for in rare circumstances, knows what they are talking about, certainly more than I do.

I've done well in reaching that goal, which means I can set another goal. I still google the side effects of medication, and that can be as harmful as googling bodily symptoms. A few weeks ago, when I had that cold in Michigan, I went to Target three times to get something for my symptoms. Three times. I kept looking for a cough and chest congestion syrup that would help but wouldn't make me feel shaky or give me palpitations. Finally, my cold got so bad that I bit the bullet and grabbed something. I took the recommended dosage in the car before heading back to the rink, but only after searching on the internet for what the potential side effects were. Half an hour later, I was feeling some of the worst side effects. In a fight against the mind and the body, the mind wins almost every time. The next step for me is to ask a pharmacist about the side effects of a medication, trust them to tell me if I should worry about them or not, and, where appropriate, take the medicine, whether it's over-the-counter or prescribed. The final level, in terms of bodily symptoms, is to be able to reach a state of mindfulness where I can observe what's going on in my body, dispassionately and non-judgmentally, and act accordingly without the interference of panic or unreasonable worry.

For each fear, there is an appropriate and rational response to work towards. You name the fear, and then you document steps that will help you address that fear. It may be only one thing that is an irrational fear for you, or it may be several, but they each require care and attention because if they go unchecked, you can find yourself spiralling into the condition I found myself in not once but twice. And really, it's affected me constantly for years, even if I've not had a nervous breakdown. I don't know what it's like to feel normal anymore. Or maybe this is normal. It's certainly become normal. If that's the prerequisite for normalcy, I suppose I feel normal. That doesn't mean I can't feel better. I can definitely feel worse if I allow my fear to control things and I don't control my fear.

It's more than that, though. It's not only fear. It's making sure that my body and mind are healthy enough to fight against anxiety and depression. And so, there's an entirely different list. You can call it a wellness list. Some of the things on this list might cross-pollinate with the list of fears and strategies, and that's perfectly fine. For example, I am afraid of exercise, but exercise will make me feel well. If I feel well, I am more ready to keep fighting. I work on one list, and then I set goals on the second list. I know that if I walk ten thousand steps per day, something totally doable, I will be healthier. Walking is healthy. If I'm healthier, I don't just feel better in the body but also in the mind. There are a few more for me that are priorities. I need to sleep better. I need to find ways that I can sleep better. And when I can't sleep, I need goals that are related to acceptance and productivity. What I mean by that is, if I wake up at 4:00 a.m., and after trying for half an hour, I cannot go back to sleep, is it best if I lay in bed and let my mind run rampant? Because it will. What if I got out of bed and did yoga? What if I had a shower, got dressed, and sat at my desk to do some work? What if I got out of bed, sat on a chair, and read something? Training myself to get back to sleep is possible, but when all else fails, I can take steps to ensure that, at least if I'm up, I'm not sinking in my own destructive thoughts.

I need to manage my time better in almost every aspect. I need to recognize what my triggers are and how to, as much as possible, avoid them. I do not like being away from home, and yet, it's impossible to avoid with the job that I have as a writer. I travel a lot, and I'm going farther away as the years go by, which means I am constantly travelling more. If I go to Hong Kong or Germany, I have to take into account the days required to get to and from these locations, along with the time I'll be doing events. If I jump at an opportunity to perform a keynote address but see that in two days I'm supposed to be somewhere else in the country, I'm presented with the choice of going home for a day and then leaving again or flying straight to the other location. I get to see the kids for a day, but I'll tire myself out. Already, in November, I'm going to be away for two weeks or more because I chose mental wellness over seeing my kids in person. Going home for a day, flying out the next morning, and coming back for another day before leaving again would take a toll on me. Instead, I'll FaceTime, text, or call, staying on the road while keeping connected. It becomes a question of value. Is the value of me being away worth the price I have to pay? The value of an out-of-town engagement can be measured from a monetary standpoint or how it will translate into book sales. The price that I pay, what I give up for that value, is mental health and well-being, including time away from family and my ability to overcome a fear of distance. If home is where

I feel safe, what do I do if I fly across the world? The lists have overlapped again. They do that. But that's how you make careful, calculated decisions.

A few years ago, I made poor decisions. I was away more than half the time, and when I got back, I crashed. Last year, I was away almost as often but handled it differently, and I made it out of that busy time virtually unscathed. I think part of the answer is realizing that money is temporary and family is permanent, so you have to put yourself and your family first. That's the priority. If you set that as a priority, you learn to make the right decisions faster. I need to support my family financially, but I also need to support them with my presence, and I *want* to support them with my presence. What are they going to remember more when I'm gone? That I was able to pick up a PlayStation 5 for my son when he moved to Texas this year, or that I hugged him at the door when I dropped him off at his billet family and told him that I loved him and that I was proud of him. He enjoys his PS5, but I'd like to think that in a few years, it'll be the latter memory he holds closer to him, more than a video game console. Will James or Lauren remember what I got them at the flea market on the weekends when they grow up? Or will they remember that Dad was there to take them, and we spent mornings together looking at antiques and vintage comics and Pokémon cards and getting a treat on the way home? Will Emily and Anna remember the souvenirs they got in Hawaii when I took them with me this year to do a school visit? Or will they remember standing on the pier with me and looking at the stars? Or sitting on the beach and watching fireworks? That's the stuff that matters. That's the important stuff.

*

Dad came to one of my events early on in my career, and I was using PowerPoint. I was reading off notes, reading off the screen, and I wasn't connecting with the audience. That's what he noticed, and he was right. I've always loved public speaking, but I've had to work at it to get good at it. I think there are some similarities between what works with family and what works with public speaking, because what we're trying to do in both cases is make connections. After that presentation, Dad told me to stop reading off notes and to start looking at people. He told me to speak from the heart. Since then, that's what I've done. I may have a picture here and there that I throw onto a screen, but I rarely have notes. If I do, they are bullet points with one or two words on each point to ensure I have some sort of guide. If I lose my train of thought or get sidetracked (I go on tangents and ramble quite often), I can refocus seamlessly and carry on without interrupting my presentation. I'd like to think that while teachers get something out of what I say, they get more out of feeling like they know me, out of the community that we build, and that makes the words stick better, too. I love the relationships that I've made with readers, teachers, and librarians, and I receive enough emails to know that they feel comfortable getting in touch with me.

I've tried to approach this story in the same way. I want you to feel comfortable, even if a lot of this can be uncomfortable. I want you to feel as if we've sat together and I've told you a story in person, sitting across from one another, face to face. There are no fancy words here. This is not literary. I've gone through some hard things. You may have gone through some hard things. You may know somebody who has gone through some hard things.

I'm still going through them, and you, or somebody you love, might be, too.

One of the most frequent topics of conversation Dad and I had was about how we were going to heal. We were concerned with Indigenous and non-Indigenous relations as well as the healing that Indigenous people have to do individually, within families, and in communities from the profound colonial trauma we have experienced, still experience today, and are likely to experience in the future, until Turtle Island gets its act together.

How do we do that? The answer is in the stories we tell and how we accept the stories that are told to us. In those stories, we come to understand, acknowledge, and appreciate what makes us unique, what makes one person differ from another without setting them apart. In those stories, we find the definition of our-selves, of everything that goes into making me who I am, includ-ing my mental health conditions, and of everything that goes into making you who you are. In those stories, we uncover similari-ties, the things between us that we share in our lived experiences and states of being. All of this builds a stronger community and extends beyond the act of reconciliation to vital issues like men-tal health. Mental health is most certainly included within the healing required from the impacts of historical trauma; just look at the epidemic of youth suicide in Indigenous communities, an epidemic we desperately need to pay better attention to. But it's something that is universal. It's cross-cultural.

In my journey, I've been gifted with community and friend-ships with people based on all of the above, with people who are on a similar journey as I am on, within the context of mental health. We cannot miss the opportunity to heal like that, to heal collectively, in support of each other, and not in silos where we are left feeling that we are alone, that we have to suffer alone, when we are not and when we do not.

There are steps in our journey that are familiar regardless of the differing obstacles we face, from how anxiety manifests itself within our bodies and minds to the roots of it all, how that seed was planted and how it has grown into the little monsters that sit on our shoulders. I have come to believe that not one worry is insurmountable, no matter how small you may think it is or how it looms over you as if you are standing in the shadow of a giant.

I live with depression that comes and goes like the tide. Anxiety is always there with me, no matter what time of day, no matter what is going on in my life, and no matter where I am. I pack it in my suitcase with my socks and shirts and jeans, both what it was and what it is.

In a lot of ways, I am still that boy who can't fall asleep at night because of the thoughts that plague me. I am still playing sixties music on my ghetto blaster, staring at the ceiling, throwing every one of those thoughts against the white paint like it's a movie screen. I am still wandering the house in the still of night, through the darkness, trying to shake the feeling of my insignificance against the enormity of infinity. I am still standing in front of the living room window, staring past the trees, past the lazy glow of the bowing streetlights, past the constellations that tell stories as beautiful as I have ever told with the written or spoken word, into the depths of oblivion, and trying to come to terms with my place in it. I am still tangled within the roots of my struggles, of my anxiety.

I think a lot about what my mother told me once about death. I talk about it because it has resonated with me. I was terrified of dying. We had just lost a family member, and I couldn't understand or comprehend how time would pass for them in a blink until we reached the end of all things. I couldn't accept that one day, the same thing would happen to me. I heard a quote recently about coping with death. It was about somebody's atheism and whether, in the face of nothingness, they were fearful. The person responded that they would feel the same about death as they did before they were born. That is to say, they will have no thoughts or feelings about it. At some point, everybody on this planet, everybody who ever was and everybody who ever will be, did not exist and will not exist, in a literal sense (depending on your belief system, of course). On the subject of death and its inevitability, my mother asked, "Doesn't it make you feel better that we're all in the same boat?"

When I was younger, I hated that she had said that. It didn't make me feel better at all. What would I know if I was dead like everybody else? But the older I get, and the closer I come to the inevitable, I feel differently about my mother's question. If a fear of mine is death, and it is, there is no overcoming that. There is no way to break down that barrier. It's coming. Every second of every day, somebody reaches the finish line. I'd like to think I'm immortal, or wish that I could play at immortality as a youth does, to have it not enter my mind at all. But that's avoidance, and avoidance is a crutch. Slowly, I've come to a place where I am sometimes able to accept what's coming and focus not on the end but on the path towards it. That's the most productive thing to do. If I were able to do that, a great deal of my anxiety would be more manageable, as so much of it is tied to my fear of death. We have an expiry date. No matter what we believe happens afterwards, it's something else we share; it is a part of the human condition.

With all of this—with everything I carry on this journey, with the little monsters and their voices, sometimes a whisper and sometimes a jet engine–decibel scream, with the challenges I have and what I need to do to face them—it's not really about the end, is it? It's about acceptance. It's about healing. It's about finding purpose. It's about supporting one another. It's about the stories we share and connect with. No, it's not about the end at all. It's about how we get there; it's about the path we choose to take. And if I can leave you with anything, it's three words.

You got this.

ACKNOWLEDGEMENTS

After writing *Black Water: Family, Legacy, and Blood Memory*, I didn't think I would write another memoir. I didn't think I *could* write another memoir; what more was there to say that would help others? Because that's what I want to do with every book I write: help. Some of my work has been more successful at achieving that goal, but I have had a clear picture going in to each project I take on of what I want it to do. When *Black Water* was published, it solidified my decision on the whole matter of memoir writing. If that book, which I love and I think Dad would have loved, took so much out of me, why would I put myself through it all over again?

But then, life took an unexpected turn.

Whether in person, via email, or through a message on social media, people who had read *Black Water* talked to me about its impact on them. They wanted to fix a relationship with somebody in their family. They had lost a parent, and the book had helped them in some way. They were living with anxiety and saw their experience reflected in mine. Whatever the reason, *Black Water* went from emptying my tank to filling it up.

Our stories, our shared experiences, are what bind us together and aid in our healing. Mental health, in particular, calls for this sense of community, as it can often be a solitary battle. With this in mind, I have reconsidered my decision. There's a saying about creating art that goes, "One for them, one for me." You write a book for readers; then you write one for yourself. I don't know that I subscribe to that approach, but either way, I can confidently say that *All the Little Monsters* is for *us*. And, in the spirit of this community, I want to express my heartfelt gratitude to those who have made this book possible.

I have mentioned Jill a lot in this story, and she probably will not like that, but I wouldn't be here without her. In the interest of brevity, so she doesn't get too mad at me, I'll leave it at that. The same goes for you, kids. On the most challenging days, you keep me going. Emily, Cole, Anna, Lauren, and James. My favourite episode from *The Simpsons* shows Homer at his dead-end job, working day in and day out in front of a sign that Mr. Burns put up that reads: "Don't forget: You're here forever." Homer tapes pictures of Maggie all over the sign to make it read, instead: "Do it for her." While I love my job, I can confidently say, "I do it for you."

I have also mentioned my father and my mother. Their main focus in raising me was to raise me to be a gentleman. I haven't always succeeded, but I will always try my best to be just that. Dad will always be my guiding light. He will always be that hand on my stomach, asking me to breathe deeply. As for Mom, what can I say? You made me believe I could be a writer, among many other things you did for me and my brothers. *You are appreciated.* (That's an inside joke, sorry.)

To my friends in the arts who walk with me on this journey, thank you for something as simple as getting me a glass of water before an event when I was panicking, or telling me that you would help carry the load if it was too heavy for me to carry on my own. I hate to say "You know who you are," but I would never have enough space to name all of you, and you genuinely do know how much you mean to me and how much you have helped me. I will say, though:

Rogers! My Gate 12 cousin. Your tireless work in mental health advocacy and our conversations about what we both live with helped give me the courage to write this memoir. Ekosani. (That's Shelagh, to clarify.)

I am grateful to the medical professionals who have helped me along the way, most of all my psychiatrist.

Thanks to Jackie Kaiser for opening many doors, walking through them with me, and letting me talk about what's going on in my head and life. You're more than an agent to me.

Thanks to all my publishers, who know very well about my mental health challenges, but of course, thanks to HarperCollins Canada for providing me the platform to share this story. I hope it helps even one person.

Jennifer Lambert, my friend and editor. I don't know what to write, and this will probably bug you because you're my editor, but I think I will keep that right there because it helps to articulate how hard it is to quantify how much you have meant to me in the writing of this memoir, as well as *Black Water* and *The Theory of Crows*. Thank you for your patience, compassion, trust, honesty, and, above all else, kindness.

Finally, I want to say something to you, the reader. If you're going through something, reach out to somebody—even me. I am easy to find.

And remember, you never know when somebody's struggling.

"Be a little kinder than you have to."
—E. Lockhart, *We Were Liars*

SOURCES

The quotation from James R. Sherman in the epigraph is from *Rejection* (Keene, NH: Pathway Books, 1982).

The quotation from Emma Stone in the epigraph is from an interview entitled "Great Minds Think Unalike: An Interview with Emma Stone," hosted by Dr. Harold S. Koplewicz for the Child Mind Institute on October 1, 2018, in New York City.

The quotation from Wilfred Buck in chapter 1 is from an interview that took place on the CBC Radio One program *Unreserved* on January 15, 2016, between Buck and host Rosanna Deerchild.

The picture book I reference and quote from in chapter 3 is *My Mama Says There Aren't Any Zombies, Ghosts, Vampires, Creatures, Demons, Monsters, Fiends, Goblins, or Things* by Judith Viorst, illustrated by Kay Chorao (New York: Atheneum Books for Young Readers, 1987; repr. Aladdin Books, 1987).

The first movie I quote from in chapter 3 is *The Great Dictator*, written and directed by Charlie Chaplin, and released in 1940.

The second movie I quote from in chapter 3 is *The Shawshank Redemption*, written and directed by Frank Darabont, and released in 1994.

The quotation from Keanu Reeves in chapter 4 is from an interview that took place on *The Late Show with Stephen Colbert*, between Reeves and Colbert, on May 11, 2019.

The song I quote from in chapter 5 is "Free" by Florence + the Machine. It was written and produced by Florence Welch and Jack Antonoff and released on April 20, 2022.

The quotation from Mel Robbins in chapter 6 is from a TikTok video posted on August 12, 2022. It appears to be a clip from a speech she gave, although I am unclear when and where this may have been.

The quotation in chapter 8 is from *The Prestige* by Christopher Priest (New York: Simon & Schuster, 1995).

The video I reference in chapter 8 about Jacksen Proell was posted on TikTok by an account called @humankind in August 2023, although I could not find the original post.

The quotation from Bill Murray in chapter 8 is from a press conference for the film *The Monuments Men* that took place in London, England, on February 11, 2014.

The quotation from Neil deGrasse Tyson in chapter 9 is from the *DEAD Talks* podcast, episode 102, "Neil deGrasse Tyson's Personal Impact With September 11th," which aired on April 21, 2023.

The quotation from Stephen Colbert in chapter 9 is from an interview that took place on CNN between Colbert and Anderson Cooper on August 17, 2019.

The quotation from chapter 9 that encapsulates my youngest daughter's character is from William Shakespeare's *A Midsummer Night's Dream*, spoken by Helena about her friend Hermia in act 3, scene 2.

The quotation in my acknowledgements is from *We Were Liars* by E. Lockhart (New York: Delacorte Press, 2014).